The American Crisis Series

Books on the Civil War Era

Steven E. Woodworth, Assistant Professor of History,
Texas Christian University
SERIES EDITOR

The Civil War was the crisis of the Republic's first century —the test, in Abraham Lincoln's words, of whether any free government could long endure. It touched with fire the hearts of a generation, and its story has fired the imaginations of every generation since. This series offers to students of the Civil War, either those continuing or those just beginning their exciting journey into the past, concise overviews of important persons, events, and themes in that remarkable period of America's history.

The Men of Secession and Civil War, 1859–1861

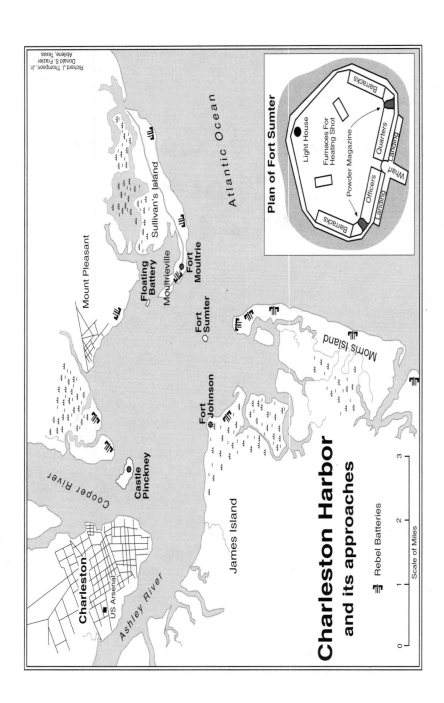

Charleston Harbor
and its approaches

Richard J. Thompson, Jr.
Donald S. Frazier
Abilene, Texas

Plan of Fort Sumter

Light House
Furnaces For Heating Shot
Powder Magazine
Barracks
Quarters
Landing
Wharf
Officers
Landing
Barracks

Atlantic Ocean

Sullivan's Island
Mount Pleasant
Floating Battery
Moultrieville
Fort Moultrie
Fort Sumter
Morris Island
Fort Johnson
Castle Pinckney
Cooper River
Charleston
US Arsenal
Ashley River
James Island

⚔ Rebel Batteries

0   1   2   3
Scale of Miles

The Men of Secession and Civil War, 1859–1861

The American Crisis Series
BOOKS ON THE CIVIL WAR ERA
NO. I

James L. Abrahamson

A Scholarly Resources Inc. Imprint
Wilmington, Delaware

Scholarly Resources Inc.
104 Greenhill Avenue
Wilmington, DE 19805-1897
www.scholarly.com

Library of Congress Cataloging-in-Publication Data

Abrahamson, James L.
    The men of secession and Civil War, 1859–1861 / James L.
Abrahamson.
        p.   cm. — (American crisis series ; no. 1)
    Includes bibliographical references (p.) and index.
    ISBN 0-8420-2818-8 (cloth : alk. paper) — ISBN 0-8420-
2819-6 (paper : alk. paper)
    1. Secession—Southern States. 2. United States—History—
Civil War, 1861–1865—Causes. 3. Southern States—Politics
and government—1775–1865. 4. United States—Politics and
government—1815–1861. I. Title. II. Series.

E459.A18   2000
973.7'13—dc21   99-089807

⊗ The paper used in this publication meets the minimum require-
ments of the American National Standard for permanence of paper for printed library materials, Z39.48, 1984.

To the memory of my

mother and father

To the American soldier and his family,

who sacrifice so much in

defense of freedom

ACKNOWLEDGMENTS

This book derives from an "Adventures in Ideas" seminar at the University of North Carolina at Chapel Hill and a similar program at the Duke University Institute for Learning in Retirement. Asked by Tom Buell to support his discussion of Civil War generalship with presentations on the coming of the war and its impact on the home front, I prepared the lecture that led, through Steve Woodworth, my exceptionally capable and encouraging general editor, to *The Men of Secession and Civil War, 1859–1861*. Long fascinated by the role of individuals in great events, I eagerly accepted the invitation of Scholarly Resources to tell the story of the prewar crisis through the lives of men whose ideas and actions, for good or ill, influenced popular attitudes and shaped the course of events.

For assistance with the research supporting this book, I thank staff members of the Davis Library, especially Paula Hinton, and the Southern Historical Collection, both at the University of North Carolina. Though the credits in the Cast of Characters identify the institutions responsible for the illustrations, that is poor recognition for the kind people in each who helped me locate and reproduce the needed photographs. Working from a document in the University of North Carolina Maps Collection, Don Frazier prepared the sketch of Charleston Harbor that appears as the frontispiece of this book.

My story of the coming of secession and the Civil War could not have been so easily or so well told without the help of the special studies and biographies described in the Bibliographical Essay at the end of the book. Though their authors are too numerous to mention again here, I wish to acknowledge at the commencement my great debt to their labors. Their insights improved my own vision; any error in the use of their research is, of course, my responsibility alone.

Tom Buell not only helped to get this project started but also remained to the end, joining Steve Woodworth and Albina and Chuck Giardino in reading and commenting on early versions of my manuscript. They were my experts and my general readers, testing the manuscript's accuracy and its appeal. I, of course, remain responsible for any errors of fact or interpretation and infelicities of expression. Matthew Hershey and Linda Pote Musumeci at Scholarly Resources provided helpful and timely guidance as well as readily cooperated with my efforts to shape the organization of the book.

Above all, I express deepest appreciation to my wife, Marigold, who encouraged me at every step of the way and ensured that I had a happy and supportive environment in which to reflect and write.

J. L. A.

The new [Confederate] constitution has put to rest, *forever*, all agitating questions relating to our peculiar institution. . . . Our new government is founded . . . , its corner-stone rests, upon the great truth that the negro [*sic*] is not equal to the white man; that slavery—subordination to the superior race—is his natural and normal condition.

Alexander Stephens
"Cornerstone" Speech
Savannah, March 1861

CONTENTS

INTRODUCTION

We seem to be drifting into destruction before
our eyes, in utter helplessness.
—Caleb Cushing, January 1860[1]

We are going to destruction as fast as we can.
—Alexander Stephens, November 1860[2]

IN SIMILAR LANGUAGE, two American statesmen—a New Englander sympathetic to the South and a Georgian who loved the
Union—lamented the course of events in the months following
John Brown's October 1859 raid on Harpers Ferry. Try as they
might, neither Caleb Cushing, by supporting Southern extremists, nor Alexander Stephens, by resisting them, could turn aside
their nation's drift toward secession and war.

Their inability to avert catastrophe derived from the greater
energy and skill of their opponents, who either thought Southern independence worth the cost of national destruction or believed preserving the Union worth the price of civil war. This
book's first premise, then, is that we cannot fully understand the
origins of the Civil War if we look only to events and to the influence of allegedly irresistible but impersonal forces. We must instead carefully consider the thoughts, words, and actions of the
individuals who shaped events or defined their meaning.

If the influence of impersonal factors associated with long-
standing tension between the slave and free areas of the United
States accounts for secession and war, we should wonder why
they did so only in 1859–1861 and not a decade sooner—or later.
Before agreeing with historians attributing the Civil War to the
operation of underlying and possibly irresistible forces, we must
insist that they explain why those forces so suddenly over-
whelmed the well-established ability of American statesmen to
effect compromise. The nation's leaders had achieved union at
the Constitutional Convention and preserved it in response to
the crisis over Missouri's statehood, during South Carolina's

failed attempt to nullify federal law, and when disposing of the territories acquired from the war with Mexico.

To be sure, many forces and circumstances of an impersonal nature did divide antebellum Americans, but not always on clear North-South lines. Differences over land and tariff policies, for instance, are better understood from the perspective of three regions: Northeast, West, and Southeast. If New England, the Midwest, and the Deep South represented different economic patterns and interests, they were as much complementary as opposed. Cultural differences can be magnified into a source of inevitable conflict only by ignoring both what Americans had in common and the great variations within states and regions. Whatever each state's dominant social class, all Americans shared similar political institutions and values as well as the same history and heroes.

There was, of course, the very great problem of slavery, which in various ways inspired secession. Even so, widespread Northern tolerance of slavery where it already existed and the low opinion of Africans shared by nearly all whites had long assisted the search for sectional compromise. Nor should it be forgotten that even in 1861 four of the slave states, with one-third of the South's white population, chose to remain within the Union, and four others held back until the Confederate attack on Fort Sumter. Slavery's relation to secession and war is no simple matter.

Fully comprehending the Union's drift into destruction requires us to look beyond circumstances and impersonal forces. We must consider individual behavior and how men, by shaping and interpreting events, intensified sectional hostility, sapped support for government, prepared their fellow citizens for secession or resistance, and overcame those advocating compromise. Even if pursued thoughtlessly or without full intention, political upheaval does not occur until a few individuals have first created a rebellious spirit within some portion of the general population. Like their forebears of 1776, who justified independence by condemning Parliamentary legislation and vilifying George III, secessionists tore at the bonds that bound Americans to one another and their government as they maligned Northerners and found sinister intent in federal policy. The Union's champions, defending it as guarantor of all they most valued, equally threatened national unity when they characterized every defense of Southern interests as a conspiracy against free society and national union. With such actions, those who would destroy a government and those who would preserve it made fearful enemies of the other and gave dreadful meaning and significance to differences they had long tolerated. In the end, they convinced their contemporaries to risk violence in defense of interests newly perceived as too vital for compromise.

A second premise of this book is that explaining the Civil War requires us to consider three distinct events: the secession of the cotton states; the refusal of Republicans to accept disunion; and the response of the upper South to that refusal. While relating those stories, each of this book's chapters focuses on the role of only a few men. They did not, by themselves, cause the Civil War, but their thoughts and actions represent the thinking and behavior of many men and illustrate how personalities shaped the course and outcome of sectional confrontation in the crisis of 1859–1861. Their personal histories also serve to remind the reader of earlier events in the life of the nation, episodes that influenced the attitudes of the men who put the nation on the path to destruction.

A NOTE ON TERMINOLOGY

Modern historians typically divide the antebellum South into three sections: 1) a Deep, Lower, or cotton South of South Carolina, Georgia, Florida, Alabama, Mississippi, Louisiana, and Texas; 2) an Upper South of Virginia, North Carolina, Tennessee, and Arkansas; and 3) a Border South of Delaware, Maryland, Kentucky, and Missouri. Antebellum Americans—and some people today—used "border" and "upper" interchangeably to identify the latter eight slave states. When referring to them collectively, I shall use upper South, dropping the capital letter to distinguish the eight from the four states of the Upper South.

NOTES

1. Cushing's January 1860 report quoted in Allan Nevins, *The Emergence of Lincoln*, vol. 2, *Prologue to Civil War, 1859–1861* (New York: Scribner's, 1950), 130.

2. Stephens's comment during the November 1860 election campaign quoted in Thomas E. Schott, *Alexander H. Stephens of Georgia: A Biography* (Baton Rouge: Louisiana State University Press, 1988), 312.

CHRONOLOGY

1820

March 3 — Missouri Compromise divides Louisiana Purchase between slave and free territories

1831

January 31 — Garrison begins publication of radical antislavery newspaper, *The Liberator*

1832 to 1833 — South Carolina's rejection of federal tariff leads to Nullification Crisis

1835 to 1836 — Texas establishes its de facto independence from Mexico, which refuses recognition

1836 to 1844 — Congressional "gag rule" denies right of petition to abolitionists

1846 to 1848 — Annexation of Texas (1845) leads to war with Mexico; ends with territorial cession to United States

1847

December 29 — Democratic presidential candidate Cass advocates Popular Sovereignty—letting residents of each territory decide status of slavery there

1850

January to September — Congress debates Compromise of 1850 concerning status of slavery in Mexican Cession and return of fugitive slaves

1854

May 30 — Kansas-Nebraska Act repeals Missouri Compromise; applies Popular Sovereignty to those two territories

1856

May to
    September
Following several fraudulent elections, civil war over slavery erupts in Kansas Territory

November 4
Republican Frémont comes in second to Democrat Buchanan in presidential contest

1857

March 6
Dred Scott decision

1858

February to
    May
Congress debates and rejects Kansas statehood under Lecompton (pro-slavery) constitution

August to
    October
Lincoln-Douglas debates

1859

October 16–18
Brown's raid on Harpers Ferry

1860

April to June
Democratic Party splits; Breckinridge and Douglas nominated. Constitutional Unionists pick Bell, and Republicans, Lincoln

November 6
Lincoln wins presidential election

1860 to 1861

December to
    February
Seven Deep South states secede from Union; other slave states reject secession

1861

January 9
South Carolina fires on Fort Sumter relief ship, *Star of the West*

February 4
Montgomery (Confederate) Convention and Washington Peace Convention convene

February 9
Having made themselves a provisional congress, Montgomery delegates name Davis president of the Confederacy

March 4	Congress sends states an amendment guaranteeing slavery within a state
	Lincoln's first inauguration
April 12	Confederate batteries fire on Fort Sumter
April 15	Lincoln calls for three-month volunteers
April 17	Confederacy declares war on Union, and Davis offers letters of marque authorizing privateers to raid Union high-seas commerce
April 19	Lincoln announces blockade of Confederate ports
April to May	Upper South states secede from Union

CAST OF CHARACTERS
The Men of Secession and War

PRELUDE TO DISUNION

John Brown
Chicago Historical Society

Though funded by several abolitionists, John Brown rejected their group's pacifism. In the Kansas Territory, he oversaw the murder of several men who supported slavery. His later seizure of Harpers Ferry alarmed and outraged the slave states because he intended to use weapons from its federal arsenal to arm escaped slaves and incite servile insurrection extending as far south as Alabama.

Southerners who regarded the violent Brown as typical of abolitionists, Republicans, and Northerners found little reason to seek sectional compromise. They might have felt better about prospects for reconciliation had they known the views of more representative Northern opponents of slavery, such as Salmon Chase. Though a leader of the radical wing of the Republican Party, he spoke for both his party and his section when he condemned Brown's violence and described African Americans as inferior.

Salmon Chase
Library of Congress

George Fitzhugh
Southern Historical Collection
Wilson Library
University of North Carolina at Chapel Hill

George Fitzhugh, an impover-ished Virginia planter living on a modest estate inherited by his wife, turned to writing to supplement his income. He took the advocacy of slavery to its logical extreme when he described Northern factory workers as wage slaves and urged the legal enslavement of all who performed manual labor for wages. His views may have influenced Lincoln's 1858 "House Divided" speech, in which the future president predicted the United States would not remain "perma-nently half *slave* and half *free. . . .* It will become *all* one thing, or *all* the other."

By declaring the Missouri Compromise unconstitutional and denying congressional authority over slavery in the territories, Chief Justice Roger Taney's 1857 decision in *Dred Scott v. Sandford* challenged the very basis of the Republican Party and seemingly provided evidence of a Slave Power conspiracy that sought to extend slavery to the territories and possibly even to the free states of the North.

Roger Taney
Photograph by Mathew Brady
Collection of the Supreme Court
of the United States

THE SECESSION CAMPAIGN

His long and fiery advocacy of Southern independence caused many of his contemporaries to consider South Carolina's Barnwell Rhett the Father of Secession. Believing that the antislavery North threatened Southern society, Rhett sought safety in secession, a Southern confederacy, and the acquisition of a Latin American slave empire. Oddly, as a young man Rhett had received legal instruction from one of South Carolina's leading critics of slavery.

Barnwell Rhett
The South Caroliniana Library
University of South Carolina

South Carolina also produced a younger generation of fire-eating politicians. The hot-tempered Lawrence Keitt accompanied Preston Brooks to the Senate chamber in 1857, where Brooks viciously caned Massachusetts senator Charles Sumner in retaliation for a speech, "The Crime against Kansas," that had maligned Brooks's elderly senatorial cousin.

Lawrence Keitt
The South Caroliniana Library
University of South Carolina

William Porcher Miles, another of Keitt's congressional colleagues from South Carolina, possessed a more even temper, though his speeches on behalf of secession urged Southerners to prepare for the violent defense of their rights.

William Porcher Miles
The South Caroliniana Library
University of South Carolina

Another violence-prone South Carolina hothead, Louis Wigfall. His taste for gambling, alcohol, and women drove him to Texas, where he became a U.S. Senator and leading advocate of disunion and a Southern confederacy. In Charleston in time for the assault on Fort Sumter, he persuaded Major Anderson to surrender his command.

Louis Wigfall
The South Caroliniana Library
University of South Carolina

Though equally sensitive to insults to the South's honor, James D. B. De Bow eschewed personal violence and used the pages of *De Bow's Review* to advocate Southern economic development and independence. A university professor and former director of the Census Bureau, De Bow joined Rhett in advocating a Latin American slave empire. To that end, he favored reopening the slave trade with Africa.

James D. B. De Bow
Library of Congress

South Carolina did not produce all the fire-eaters. An early advocate of scientific agriculture, Virginia's Edmund Ruffin came late to secession, but in the 1850s he tirelessly promoted it in articles, novels, speeches, letters, and conversations. After the raid on Harpers Ferry, Ruffin sent one of John Brown's pikes to each Southern governor as an indication of what the North had in mind for the slave states. To see Brown hanged, Ruffin marched with the cadets of the Virginia Military Institute, and he joined the Palmetto Guards to fire a shot at Fort Sumter.

Edmund Ruffin
Southern Historical Collection
Wilson Library
University of North Carolina at Chapel Hill

Beverley Tucker
Muscarelle Museum of Art
The College of William and Mary
in Virginia, Gift of Janet Coleman
Kimbrough and Cynthia Coleman
Moorehead, 1938.013

Another Virginian, Beverley Tucker, began attacking the Union after the 1820 Missouri Compromise, by which Congress barred slavery from most of the Louisiana Purchase. Before his death in 1851, Tucker used the Chair of Law at the College of William and Mary to condemn Thomas Jefferson's views on natural rights and to educate a generation of Southern leaders in the virtues of secession and the dangers of federal power.

Born in Rhinebeck, New York, John Quitman left for Mississippi by way of Ohio in his early twenties. Within five years, he owned a plantation and slaves and had become a disciple of South Carolina nullifier John Calhoun. After serving as a major general in the war with Mexico, he was elected governor of Mississippi and with South Carolina governor Whitemarsh Seabrook tried to take both their states out of the Union in protest of the Compromise of 1850.

John Quitman
Southern Historical Collection
Wilson Library
University of North Carolina at Chapel Hill

Though born in Georgia to a South Carolina father, William Yancey, Alabama's leading fire-eater, spent his childhood in the upstate New York home of his minister stepfather, an abolitionist. Back in South Carolina he married well and headed for Alabama to become a planter. Failing in that endeavor, he turned to law, journalism, and politics. In 1848 he first advanced the radically pro-Southern Alabama Platform that he used in 1860 to shatter the Democratic Party.

William Yancey
Southern Historical Collection
Wilson Library
University of North Carolina at Chapel Hill

A New Englander raised in New York's "burned over" district, Stephen Douglas headed for Illinois at age twenty. A Jacksonian Democrat married into a slaveowning North Carolina family, the Little Giant did his best to appease the South. As a U.S. Senator he repeatedly tried to compromise sectional conflict over territorial slavery. Southern radicals nevertheless split the Democratic Party in 1860 rather than see him nominated for the presidency.

Stephen Douglas
Southern Historical Collection
Wilson Library
University of North Carolina at Chapel Hill

Though scion of a family that regarded slavery as an evil, John Breckinridge became the 1860 presidential nominee of the Southern Democratic Party. His ambivalence about slavery did not keep him from supporting efforts to establish it in the territories—to include attempting to force it on unwilling Kansans. In 1861 he tried to take Kentucky out of the Union. He later accepted a commission in the Confederate army and served the Confederacy as secretary of war.

John Breckinridge
Southern Historical Collection
Wilson Library
University of North Carolina at Chapel Hill

Tennessee's John Bell employed several hundred slaves in his mines and rolling mill, but he took positions condemned by Southern radicals when he opposed the Mexican War, played a key role in passage of the Compromise of 1850, voted against the Kansas-Nebraska Act, and opposed efforts to force slavery into the Kansas Territory. Having long sought to preserve the Union by quieting the controversy over slavery, he readily accepted the Constitutional Union Party's presidential nomination in 1860.

John Bell
Southern Historical Collection,
Wilson Library
University of North Carolina at Chapel Hill

As a critic of Southern radicals and an opponent of secession, Alexander Stephens seemed a strange choice for Confederate vice president. Humble origins and crippling physical disabilities had not, however, kept Little Aleck from becoming one of Georgia's most respected politicians. Believing the Democratic Party better served Southern interests than did independence, he supported Douglas in 1860 and regarded Lincoln as someone whom the South could trust.

Alexander Stephens
Library of Congress

Jefferson Davis
Southern Historical Collection
Wilson Library
University of North Carolina at Chapel Hill

West Point graduate, former army officer, Mexican War hero, congressional advocate of Southern rights, and former secretary of war, the handsome Jefferson Davis of Mississippi struck secession delegates meeting in Montgomery as the ideal leader of their new nation. Few knew he suffered from periodic recurrences of malaria and excruciating, even blinding, eruptions of herpes simplex in his left eye. Worse yet, his obsession for detail undermined his capacity as an administrator, and he found it almost impossible to work closely with intelligent, self-confident men not easily bent to his will.

THE ROAD TO WAR

Believing slavery an evil barred by Nature from the western territories, Kentucky senator John Crittenden regarded the fight over slavery as unnecessary and malign. Hoping to prevent a crisis born of a Republican victory, he offered the Constitutional Union Party's John Bell as an alternative to Lincoln in the North and Breckinridge in the South. When that effort failed and secession began, Crittenden hoped his compromise would reconstruct the Union.

John Crittenden
Chicago Historical Society

Though born in Kentucky to Southern parents, grown to maturity among Southern immigrants in Indiana and Illinois, and married into a slaveowning family, Abraham Lincoln was seen as evil incarnate by Southern radicals, who made his election a justification for secession. Hoping to play for time and hold the federal forts still in his government's hands, Lincoln attempted a peaceful reprovisioning of Fort Sumter but triggered the attack for which the Confederacy had long prepared.

Abraham Lincoln
Southern Historical Collection
Wilson Library
University of North Carolina at Chapel Hill

In Tennessee, Andrew Johnson led the unionists' fight against secession, which he condemned as an attack by planters on the rights of Southern yeomen. A former tailor and governor, Senator Johnson kept his state in the Union until the Confederate attack on Fort Sumter and Lincoln's call for troops. Defeat turned to triumph, however, when Union forces reached Nashville in 1862 and Lincoln named him Tennessee's military governor and then, in 1864, his vice president.

Andrew Johnson
Southern Historical Collection
Wilson Library
University of North Carolina at Chapel Hill

While his struggle on behalf of the yeomen of northwestern Virginia put John Letcher on the path to his state's governorship, he lacked their unconditional support for the Union. Playing a major role in calling the Washington Peace Conference, Letcher stood by the Union only until reconciliation failed, and he then pursued a border state confederation until the attack on Fort Sumter put Virginia into the Confederacy. In Virginia's northwest, however, unionists arranged their own separation as the loyal state of West Virginia.

John Letcher
Museum of the Confederacy
Richmond, Virginia

PART ONE

PRELUDE TO DISUNION

"A house divided against itself cannot stand."
I believe this government cannot endure,
permanently half *slave* and half *free*.
I do not expect the Union to be *dissolved*—I do not
expect the house to *fall*—but I *do* expect
it will cease to be divided.
It will become *all* one thing, or *all* the other.
—Abraham Lincoln, June 1858*

AS THE 1850S drew to a close the American people were becoming a house divided. The residents of each section increasingly distrusted and feared their fellow citizens beyond the Ohio River and the Mason-Dixon Line. Whether advocates of free labor or defenders of chattel slavery, they regarded the other section's economic and social systems as threatening to their own. Both sections, moreover, contained extremists seemingly unwilling to rest until they had laid waste the most fundamental values and institutions of the other and imposed upon it, either by law or by violence, an unwanted way of life.

To understand that mistrust and the extent to which it rested on misperception, we can look to the lives and actions of four men. Though Ohio's Salmon Chase rather than the violent John Brown represented the radical wing of the Republican Party, many Southerners had come to regard all Republicans—even all Northerners—as bloodthirsty abolitionists and racial amalgamationists who were eager, like Brown, to invade the South in support of slave insurrection. Alarmed by Chief Justice Roger Taney's

*From Abraham Lincoln's June 1858 "House Divided" speech, with his emphasis and, in quotation marks, his version of a Biblical passage, quoted in David H. Donald, *Lincoln* (London: Jonathan Cape, 1995), 206.

1

proslavery interpretation of the Constitution and a Democratic president's attempt to force slavery on unwilling Kansans, Northerners too grew fearful. Perhaps the ravings of extremists such as George Fitzhugh would encourage slavery's advocates to push the institution throughout all the United States, even onto all Americans who worked with their hands, whatever their race.

CHAPTER ONE

JOHN BROWN, SALMON CHASE, AND THE SOUTHERN RESPONSE TO AMERICAN ANTISLAVERY

We have here only one life to live, and once
to die; and if we lose our lives it will perhaps
do more for the cause than our lives would be
worth in any other way.
—John Brown, October 1859[1]

SHORTLY AFTER SUNSET on Sunday, October 16, 1859, the men left the old Kennedy place in western Maryland headed for Harpers Ferry, seven miles distant, across the Potomac River in nearby Virginia.[2] John Brown drove the wagon with its load of pikes and tools. Most of his raiders—thirteen whites and five blacks, each carrying a Sharps rifle and two revolvers—followed him two-by-two down the narrow road. Three other raiders—all white—remained at the farmhouse. They would secure the group's base before moving the rest of the 950 pikes, 198 Sharps rifles, and 200 revolvers to a schoolhouse a mile short of the village. With them, Brown planned to arm the free blacks, escaped slaves, and abolitionists whom he expected to join his Provisional Army once it had raised the standard of insurrection on Virginia's soil.

To seize the federal arsenal, block the bridges into town, and terrify its residents into submission, Brown relied upon surprise, not size. No federal troops were in the area, and he believed that taking hostages would hold local militia at bay while word of the attack spread through the countryside and brought slavery's opponents to his relief. Enlarged and well armed, his newly formed army would then escape to the nearby mountains and carry the attack on slavery as far south as Alabama, liberating slaves as it went. If his plan had any deficiencies, God would compensate by confounding Brown's enemies, shielding his men from danger, and ensuring success. If not, perhaps failure better served the divine purpose.

As Brown's party moved along the canal that paralleled the Potomac, John Cook and Charles Tidd left the group to cut the telegraph lines east and west of town. Approaching the wagon-and-railroad bridge, Brown signaled to John Kagi and Aaron Stevens, who sped across it to capture the night watchman as others raced to secure the Shenandoah River bridge. Leaving four sentinels to guard their first two objectives, the remaining raiders slipped past the Wager House, a hotel serving as railroad station, to seize the government arsenal and armory, where they caught the watchman by surprise before making prisoners of the few people in the nearby streets. Brown then led a party to Hall's Rifle Works a half mile distant, easily taking it and seizing another prisoner. Kagi along with John Copeland and Lewis Leary, two free blacks from Oberlin, Ohio, remained to hold the rifle works.

Without encountering any resistance or rousing the town, Brown's raiders had taken all of their initial objectives—and a vast amount of arms and munitions. Once Owen, one of Brown's sons, had moved the raiders' weapons cache from the farmhouse, Virginians and Marylanders eager to join the assault on slavery could pick up arms at the school, from Oliver Brown, another son, at the Shenandoah bridge, or from Kagi at the rifle works. With all going well, Brown also ordered a detachment into the countryside to take hostages, the most prominent among them Colonel Lewis W. Washington, a planter and great-grandnephew of the first president. All were put under guard in the armory's fire-engine house. Well armed and protected by those prisoners, Brown's men might have made their escape.

Anticipating a flood of new supporters, Brown instead tarried in Harpers Ferry, where his men soon fired on a relief watchman, giving him a head wound that sent him hurrying back to the Wager House. Alerted to the danger by the injured watchman and fired upon by Brown's sentinels guarding a barrier at the Potomac bridge, the engineer of the 1 A.M. express passing through Harpers Ferry from Wheeling moved his train back to the station. As it retreated, Hayward Shepherd, a free black and the station's baggage master, came down the tracks in search of the watchman. For retreating when ordered to halt, Shepherd received a mortal wound from Brown's sentinels, thus tragically making an African American the raid's first victim. All the commotion awakened a few townsmen, and at about dawn Brown's men fatally shot Thomas Boerley, one of the more curious. Soon the bell of the town's Lutheran church tolled "insurrection," and nearby churches spread the alarm, as did the express train when Brown allowed it to move on at 5 A.M.

Still, Brown hesitated. To his dismay, no antislavery men or escaped slaves had yet arrived to reinforce his raiders, though hastily assembled militia companies of fearful and outraged Virginians poured into town and began firing on the rifle works and engine house. Confounded by the militia's speedy response and the failure of anyone to rally to his cause, Brown seemed incapable of decision when Kagi, at the distant rifle works, pleaded for the raiders to abandon the town before becoming surrounded. Further scattering his forces, Brown instead sent three of his men and several "liberated" slaves to help Owen transfer the weapons from the Kennedy farm.

While Brown delayed, militia from Charlestown drove his men from the Potomac and Shenandoah bridges at noon and then seized the heights above Harpers Ferry and occupied the Wager House. Fleeing the bridges, Brown's son Oliver and another sentinel made it back to the armory, but former slave Dangerfield Newby, who had joined Brown in hopes of freeing his wife and children held in slavery in Virginia, became the first of the raiders to die. Revealing much about the local state of mind, one townsman made trophies of Newby's ears while others beat his lifeless body with sticks.

Nearly surrounded, cut off from his rearguard in Maryland, separated from Kagi at the rifle works, and with two men dispatched to hold the arsenal, Brown at last thought of escape. He sent Will Thompson and one of the hostages under a white flag to negotiate the release of his prisoners in exchange for free passage out of Virginia. The crowd instead seized Thompson. Brown, growing desperate, sent Watson, the third of his sons participating in the raid, Aaron Stevens, and the armory superintendent under a second flag of truce. The mob promptly shot both raiders, though Watson crawled back to the engine house and one of

Brown's prisoners heroically carried Stevens to the railroad station for medical attention.

With the militiamen and locals fast becoming a drunken, bloodthirsty rabble unwilling to negotiate, Brown's scheme collapsed. Panicked, William Leeman, the youngest raider, was shot down as he fled to an islet in the Potomac. There his body lay for several hours, a target for the militia sharpshooters. Other locals drove out the three raiders at the rifle works, killing Kagi and Leary and taking Copeland prisoner. Only the arrival of a local physician prevented the townsmen from lynching Copeland, a black man from North Carolina. When Edwin Coppac, one of the Quakers among Brown's raiders, mistakenly shot the mayor, several townsmen dragged Will Thompson from the Wager House, shot him in the head, and dumped his body in the river, where it too became a target for vengeful Virginians.

By the end of the day, a new militia company from Martinsburg arrived to cut off Brown's last possible avenue out of the armory, but not before the two men holding the arsenal made their escape. John Cook, who had lived in the town for a time as Brown's spy, saw the raiders' plight and made his way to the schoolhouse to warn its men to flee. Surrounded, with most of his men dead, wounded, or scattered, Brown seemed to have failed utterly; no escaped slave or white abolitionist had enlisted for his armed assault on slavery.

As the railroad carried more militia companies to Harpers Ferry, President James Buchanan learned of the raid. He promptly dispatched the soldiers of three artillery batteries, ninety marines led by Lieutenant Israel Green, and two cavalry officers, Lieutenant J. E. B. Stuart and Colonel Robert E. Lee, who took command of all forces late Monday night. For Brown's remaining raiders, the end came the next morning when the marines rushed the engine house as Stuart, under a flag of truce, delivered Lee's demand to surrender. The resistance of the unwounded raiders quickly collapsed when the marines bayoneted Jeremiah Anderson and Dauphin Thompson, and Lieutenant Green struck old Brown with his dress sword.

～⁓ News of the Harpers Ferry raid and Brown's aims horrified an already fearful South.[3] It now imagined the North filled with hordes of unrelenting abolitionists and cunning Republicans, all bent on inciting servile insurrection with the possible assistance of slaveless Southern whites resentful of the planters' dominance. Better informed Southerners rejected such fears. Secessionist James Seddon, for example, warned Senator Robert M. T. Hunter, a fellow Virginian, that Brown's "squalid foray" represented no more than the "mad folly of a few deluded cranks," whom the South should avoid turning into "heroes and martyrs" by making too much of the whole affair. After helping the Senate investigate the raid, Mississippi senator Jefferson Davis described the raid as no more than "the act of lawless ruffians, under the sanction of no public or political authority." The Richmond newspapers agreed, heaping derision on the incompetence of Brown and his men, who had failed to draw a single Virginian—black or white—to their cause.[4]

Had Northerners universally and vigorously condemned the attack, they might have reassured less confident Southerners, whom historian Allan Nevins described as eager to believe that only "the more malignant abolitionists would express sympathy for treason, servile insurrection, and murder."[5] In Boston and New York, conservatives tried to meet Southern expectations by holding meetings condemning the raid, approving Brown's death sentence, expressing contempt for his financial backers, and supporting the right of Virginians to own slaves. Elsewhere, both Abraham Lincoln and William Seward, his rival for leadership of the Republican Party, repudiated the raid, with Lincoln adding that opposition to slavery could not "excuse violence, bloodshed and treason." So "absurd" was Brown's plan, even slaves withheld their support because they "saw plainly enough that it could not succeed." Seward approved Brown's hanging as "necessary and just," and the next year's Republican platform characterized the Harpers Ferry attack as "among the gravest of crimes."[6]

Such efforts to soothe the South nevertheless failed to overcome the appeal of the dignified and heroic conduct shown by Brown between the time of his arrest and his execution. Suffering from painful wounds, the deaths of two sons, and the utter defeat of his hopes, Brown calmly justified his actions and charged his first interrogators, Virginia governor Henry Wise and senator James M. Mason, with "a great wrong against God and humanity.

. . . It would be perfectly right for any one to interfere with you so far as to free those you wil[l]fully and wickedly hold in bondage." Relying on the Golden Rule, Brown affirmed his "pity [for] the poor in bondage that have none to help them: that is why I am here; not to gratify any personal animosity, revenge, or vindictive spirit. It is my sympathy with the oppressed and the wronged, that are as good as you and as precious in the sight of God."[7]

Though some considered Brown a madman, a letter to his wife explains why he shrewdly refused all efforts either to rescue him or to spare his life on grounds of insanity. "I have been *whip[p]ed*," he wrote, "but am sure I can recover all the lost capital occasioned by the disaster, by only hanging a few moments by the neck; & I feel quite determined to make the utmost possible out of a defeat."[8]

With Brown embracing the gallows, leading abolitionists demonstrated their skill as propagandists when they resolved to make good use of his death. Thomas Wentworth Higginson wrote that "acquittal or rescue would [not] do half as much good as his being executed," and Henry David Thoreau "almost fear[ed] to hear of his deliverance, doubting if a prolonged life, if any life, can do as much good as his death." Helping Brown to snatch victory from his debacle, William Lloyd Garrison, editor of the radical abolitionist *Liberator*, called upon his countrymen to make "the day of [Brown's] execution . . . the occasion of such a public moral demonstration against the bloody and merciless slave system as the land has never witnessed."[9]

Many Northerners, admiring Brown's fortitude and sympathetic to his cause if not his methods, responded. On December 2, 1859, the North went into mourning. Church bells tolled to mark a martyr's passing; citizens hung black bunting, fired cannon, attended prayer meetings, and adopted memorial resolutions. Boston, New York, and Philadelphia held large public meetings, at one of which Garrison, though a pacifist, wished "success to every slave insurrection at the South." Thoreau, calling Brown "an angel of light," compared him to Christ, and Ralph Waldo Emerson predicted that his death would "make the gallows as glorious as the cross." As pilgrims later flocked to Brown's grave in North Elba, New York, publishers rushed a biography into print and circulated great numbers of lithographs of Brown's likeness. According to the Lawrence *Republican*, "It is safe to say that the death of no man in America has ever produced so profound a sensation. The feeling of deep and sorrowful indignation seems to possess the masses."[10]

That was not at all the reaction for which Southern conservatives had hoped. Misunderstanding the North's intent, South Carolina's Christopher Memminger declared: "Every village bell which tolled its solemn note at the execution of Brown proclaims to the South the approbation of that village of insurrection and servile war."[11] Such conclusions, reinforced by the discovery that six of the Northeast's most prominent cultural leaders, all abolitionists, had given Brown financial support, caused many Southerners to begin looking to their defenses and measuring the risks of remaining in the Union. Fearful Southern legislators appropriated funds for the purchase of arms and the expansion of militias. New laws restricted the movement of free blacks, and masters kept a closer watch on slaves as counties increased patrols. Anyone from the North—teachers, ministers, traveling merchants—faced suspicion, and those daring to criticize slavery might be whipped, tarred, feathered, ridden out of town on a rail, ordered to leave the state, or even hanged. The British consul in Charleston characterized the situation in that city as a reign of terror.

Seeing only enemies to their north, Southerners fell prey to the calls of those urging them to reconsider their relation to the federal government. The editor of the Baltimore *Sun* proclaimed his refusal to "live under a government, the majority of whose subjects or citizens regard John Brown as a martyr and a Christian hero." Farther south, the Richmond *Whig* asserted that "recent events have wrought almost a complete revolution in the sentiments, the thoughts, the hopes, of the oldest and steadiest conservatives in all the Southern states."[12]

Advocates of secession encouraged those views. They saw in Brown's raid and the Northern reaction an opportunity to revive their faltering movement, unify the South, and break its ties to the Union. Misinterpreting this Northern reaction, James D. B. De Bow pushed for Southern independence when he advised readers of the January 1860 edition of his *Review* that the North "has sanctioned and applauded theft, murder, treason, and at the hands of our Northern Brethren, has shed Southern Blood on Southern soil! There is—there can be no peace!"[13] That the Senate's investigation of the raid, chaired by Virginia's James Mason with Jefferson Davis as chief inquisitor, found no evidence of widespread conspiracy or Republican involvement made no difference to radicals such as De Bow. By mid-1860, as the Republican platform repudiated John Brown and secessionist Edmund Ruffin lamented that the "violent agitation & impulse caused by the Harper's Ferry affair seem[ed] to have completely subsided,"[14] secessionists still labored to convince the South that Brown, abolitionists, and Black Republicans were one and the same and entirely representative of Northern opinion. The South's safety, they shouted, lay in disunion.

∼ Within two years' time, many of the men who joined in De Bow's condemnation of the North would produce tragic consequences. Before accepting the accuracy of their criticisms and the inevitability of the direction in which they led, we should give some attention to Northern attitudes. For abolitionists were not so violence prone as perceived in the South, and few Republicans—or Northerners—shared their views or wanted even to have much to do with them.

Abolitionists, perhaps only 1 percent of the Northern population, constituted a very small group seeking to end slavery throughout the United States. Rather than do so violently, as pacifists they aimed to abolish bondage by persuading slaveowners of its sinfulness. The movement's more radical members went further and sought as well to change Northern racial attitudes, which denied most free blacks access to public education, the courts, and the voting booth. At the movement's extreme edge, abolitionists even attacked the Constitution as a compact with evil and trumped Southern radicals by advocating disunion to end the free states' association with sin.

Extremely unpopular when their movement emerged in the 1830s, abolitionist leaders frequently found their lives and property threatened by local mobs. After the 1837 murder of antislavery newspaperman Elijah Lovejoy, many abolitionists consequently moderated their pacifism sufficiently to justify self-defense. With passage of the 1850 Fugitive Slave Act, some also accepted that violence might result when they assisted runaways or engaged in civil disobedience to block the act's enforcement. By the mid-1850s a very few even thought it acceptable to fund men such as John Brown, then using armed force on behalf of antislavery residents caught up in the civil war raging in the Kansas Territory. Despite that evolution of abolitionist pacifism, only a few individuals on the movement's fringes—men like Brown—advocated violence, though many expected that Southern slavery would end in servile insurrection.

Far from having the North's support, abolitionists were roundly condemned by most of its Democrats, who freely stigmatized all those who opposed slavery by calling them abolitionists. Republicans, to avoid association with a discredited group, took pains to keep their distance. Beyond distaste for slavery, even their party's radical wing had little in common with abolitionism, nor did it justify Brown's methods. Ohio's senator and former governor Salmon Chase, a leading antislavery radical, regarded him as "sadly misled." Despite Brown's "bravery" and "unselfish desire to set free the oppressed," Chase unhesitatingly condemned the Harpers Ferry raid as a "criminal" attempt to "stir up insurrection[,] which if successful would deluge the land with blood and make void the fairest hopes of mankind."[15]

Had such Republican—and Northern—thinking penetrated the antebellum South, the 1860s might have had a different history. Some brief attention to Chase's career should acquaint us with the views of the Republican Party's left wing and how most Northerners felt about slavery. Chase's opposition to slavery, for example, did not extend to abolitionism and rested on different grounds. Believing Africans racially inferior to whites, he could not envisage an integrated society, and as a young man he had joined the American Colonization Society, which aimed to relocate free blacks outside the United States, a policy abhorrent to abolitionists and blacks alike. Until the country had become uniformly white, however, the humanitarian Chase worked to protect Ohio's black population from the worst forms of racial discrimination. When accepting a silver pitcher from Cincinnati's black community for his efforts, Chase made clear his intentions when he explained that his concern was not for blacks as a "separate and distinct class" but for the civil rights of all citizens.[16]

An attack on those rights in 1836 caused Chase to strengthen his opposition to slavery. In that year an anti-abolitionist mob, inspired by Cincinnati merchants with commercial ties to Kentucky and Virginia, destroyed the press of James Birney's abolitionist newspaper and then descended on his home. Regarding as "comparatively light" any harm done by men like Birney, and fearing to see his city ruled by the "mob spirit,"[17] Chase courageously stood in the editor's doorway and faced down the crowd, even though the abolitionist and his family had already fled. On principle willing to defend the liberties of those advocating unpopular causes, Chase then brought suit against the mob's leaders on behalf of Birney and his printer. He took a more active antislavery position when he later represented Birney against a criminal charge—harboring a fugitive—when it developed that a very fair-complexioned woman employed in his home was, unbeknown to him, an escaped slave.

When defending the rights of whites drew Chase into a number of fugitive-slave cases, he learned from his research that the nation's Founders, including many who owned slaves, had thought slavery an evil. Embarrassed by its incompatibility with the Declaration of Independence, they had kept the word out of the Constitution and later put their principles into action by barring slavery from the Northwest Territory. In Chase's view, "The Constitution had found slavery and left it a State institution— the creature and dependent of State law—wholly local in its existence and character" and not a "national institution."[18]

Federal law might not, therefore, sustain it. Referring to the Fifth Amendment ban on taking anyone's "life, liberty, or property, without due process of law," Chase concluded that the federal government had full authority—indeed, an obligation—to block the establishment of slavery in the territories.[19] That being so, legislation that extended slavery, such as the 1820 Missouri Compromise, the Compromise of 1850, and the 1854 Kansas-Nebraska Act, proved to Chase's satisfaction that a Slave Power had arisen to set aside the nation's commitment to freedom. Even so, in a conclusion that might have put Southern minds at ease,

Chase and the Republican platform maintained that the federal government had no power to interfere with slavery within a state.

Formerly a member of two minor antislavery parties, Chase did occasionally get ahead of his fellow Republicans, as when he maintained that the Fifth Amendment also barred Congress from permitting slavery in the District of Columbia. Nor for the same reason might the government, in his view, permit slaves to move in interstate trade, an activity under the regulatory authority of Congress. With his legal brief in the fugitive-slave cases in mind, Chase also argued that once a slave set foot outside a slave state, he became a free man. Though to some abolitionists that conclusion justified massive civil disobedience to block enforcement of the Fugitive Slave Act, Chase condemned such behavior as a threat to the law and to good social order, always his top priorities.

In his use of legal and historical reasoning, Chase had moved American antislavery beyond the abolitionists' moral and religious critique of the South's peculiar institution. In so doing, he also engaged Northerners who denigrated both blacks and abolitionists. Had radical propaganda not obscured fact, his position on federal authority might nevertheless have reassured planters that their human property was safe from Washington's interference so long as it remained within their state's jurisdiction. Chase put them on the defensive, however, by making them members of an allegedly aggressive Slave Power aiming to dominate the federal government, frustrate the Founders' intentions, and undermine the rights of free white citizens. Though not in the manner of John Brown, Chase's crusade against slavery clearly threatened Southern interests. Even so, Chase's interpretation of the Constitution, together with his racial views, provided a better basis for sectional compromise than the horrifying picture of Northern attitudes painted by secessionists and embodied in Brown's raid on Harpers Ferry.

How, then, did Republicans—and most Northerners— view slavery? Despite the fact that decades of sectional conflict unavoidably drew many to oppose it, or at least to resist its further extension, the North's principal focus was never antislavery but rather what historian Eric Foner has defined as "free labor," which he placed "at the center of the Republican ideology."[20] Within the laboring class, antebellum Northerners included farmers, craftsmen, and small businessmen as well as youthful wage earners striving to achieve economic independence. Though Abraham Lincoln hastened the steps anticipated by the ideology, he well expressed the Northern expectation that "the man who labored for another last year, this year labors for himself, and next year . . . will hire others to labor for him." Appealing both to the members of the North's middle class, who had often risen in that manner, and to its workingmen, who hoped to, Republicans extolled the dignity of labor and pledged themselves to keep open the opportunity to advance economically and thereby rise socially. Such "advancement, improvement of condition," Lincoln described as "the order of things in a society of equals."[21]

To Republicans, slavery's significance derived from its capacity to threaten that progress. Based upon the travels of the party's leaders, reports of private citizens, and experiences of Southern emigrants, Republicans described the South as the very antithesis of Northern free-labor society. Praising the dynamic Northern economy and its opportunities for advancement, an Iowa legislator reported in 1857 that "slavery . . . drove me from my native state. . . . Slavery withers and blights all it touches . . . ; it is a curse upon the poor, free, laboring white man." As a Kentucky opponent of slavery, Cassius Clay, told an Ohio audience: "The northern laboring man could, and frequently did, rise above the condition [into] which he was born [and ascend] to the first rank of society and wealth; but [I] never knew such an instance in the South."[22]

Republicans had a ready explanation for Clay's observation. According to them, a slave economy created few opportunities to advance beyond agricultural labor. It also robbed that labor of its dignity because Southerners looked down not only on slaves but also on all those who worked with their hands. From those observations, it followed that the United States must restrict slave society in order to fulfill its obligations to the common man. Should slavery not only survive but also spread to the American West, both factory workers in the East and new arrivals from abroad would refuse to go there, where they would face degrading competition from slave labor. Unable to take up new farms and open new workshops in the West, they could not rise. By remaining in the East they would increase its supply of labor, which would pull down wages and worsen their condition. A stagnant trans-Mississippi slave economy would also mean reduced demand for the East's manufactured goods, a further drag on wages.

Caring little about the ways in which slavery injured blacks, Republicans also maintained that the planter aristocracy created a hierarchical social order unsuited to political democracy. If the United States wished to preserve the North's middle-class society and continue serving as a global model of self-government, Republicans concluded they must oppose the extension of slavery as a barrier to an undemocratic and dominating Slave Power.

By regarding blacks as inferior and offering them no new rights, by guaranteeing slavery where it existed, and by keeping the territories white and leaving race relations elsewhere undisturbed, Republicans managed to propose limits on slavery while escaping the stigma of abolitionism. At least in the North they did. Schooled by ardent secessionists to ignore the very different perspectives from which John Brown, abolitionists, and Republicans viewed slavery, the South regarded the North as determined not only to bar slavery from the territories but also to bring its peculiar institution to an immediate, and possibly violent, end wherever it existed. Often equally blinded to nuance, Northerners feared the vigorous Southern defense of slavery. For them, the Supreme Court's *Dred Scott* decision of 1857 and the writings of Southern extremists proved the existence of a vast Slave Power conspiracy determined to establish slavery in the territories as well as in the free states of the North.

NOTES

1. Brown's pre-raid admonition to his Harpers Ferry "army" quoted in Stephen B. Oates, *To Purge This Land with Blood: A Biography of John Brown* (New York: Harper & Row, 1970), 289.

2. For the most part, this chapter's description of John Brown's raid and execution is drawn from ibid., 229–361.

3. This summary of the reaction to Brown's raid relies upon David M. Potter, *The Impending Crisis, 1848–1861* (New York: Harper &

Row, 1976); Allan Nevins, *The Emergence of Lincoln*, vol. 2, *Prologue to Civil War, 1859–1861* (New York: Scribner's, 1950); and several of the essays in Paul Finkelman, ed., *His Soul Goes Marching On: Responses to John Brown and the Harpers Ferry Raid* (Charlottesville: University Press of Virginia, 1995).

4. Seddon quoted in Peter Wallenstein, "Incendiaries All: Southern Politics and the Harpers Ferry Raid" in Finkelman, *Soul Goes Marching On*, 167, and Nevins, *Emergence of Lincoln*, 103; Davis quoted in William C. Davis, *Jefferson Davis: The Man and His Hour* (New York: HarperCollins, 1991), 277; on early statements by Richmond papers see Wallenstein, "Incendiaries," 150–52.

5. Nevins, *Emergence of Lincoln*, 102.

6. Lincoln, Seward, and the Republican platform quoted in Potter, *Impending Crisis*, 372 and 380.

7. Oates, *Purge This Land*, 304–5.

8. Brown to his wife quoted in Potter, *Impending Crisis*, 376.

9. Higginson, Thoreau, and the *Liberator* quoted in ibid., 376n and 378–79.

10. Emerson, Thoreau, and Garrison quoted in ibid., 379–80; *Republican* quoted in Oates, *Purge This Land*, 356.

11. Memminger quoted in Potter, *Impending Crisis*, 383.

12. Baltimore *Sun* and Richmond *Whig* quoted in ibid., 384.

13. De Bow quoted in Oates, *Purge This Land*, 323.

14. Ruffin quoted in Eric H. Walther, *The Fire-Eaters* (Baton Rouge: Louisiana State University Press, 1992), 261.

15. Chase quoted in Oates, *Purge This Land*, 311, and Frederick J. Blue, *Salmon P. Chase: A Life in Politics* (Kent, OH: Kent State University Press, 1987), 119; the latter is the basis of the following paragraphs on the Republican leader.

16. Chase quoted in ibid., 39.

17. Chase quoted in ibid., 31.

18. Chase quoted in Eric Foner, *Free Soil, Free Labor, Free Men: The Ideology of the Republican Party before the Civil War* (London: Oxford University Press, 1970), 76.

19. Fifth Amendment, U.S. Constitution.

20. Foner, *Free Soil*, 9. On Republican and Northern political ideology as described in this chapter see ibid., 11–72.

21. Lincoln quoted in ibid., 16 and 30.

22. Iowa legislator and Clay quoted in ibid., 42 and 48.

CHAPTER TWO

GEORGE FITZHUGH, ROGER TANEY, AND THE NORTHERN RESPONSE TO SOUTHERN PROSLAVERY

One set of ideas will govern and control
after awhile the civilized world. Slavery
will every where be abolished, or every where
be re-instituted.
—George Fitzhugh, *Sociology for the South*[1]

[Negroes] had no rights which the white man
was bound to respect.
—Roger Taney, *Dred Scott v. Sandford*[2]

JUST AS THE antislavery violence of John Brown outraged the South, the verbal assaults of slavery advocates such as George Fitzhugh fed Northern belief in an aggressive Slave Power. The most singular of the proslavery writers, Fitzhugh, like Brown, achieved such fame as he would know in the 1850s after first showing as little aptitude for the law as Brown did for business.[3] Member of a prominent but financially distressed Virginia family, the self-educated Fitzhugh practiced law in desultory fashion and fathered nine children while living in his wife's home, "situated on the fag-end of a once noble estate" near Port Royal.[4] Though slavery's advocate rather than its enemy, Fitzhugh shared Brown's willingness to offend the American public by attacking even revered and fundamental beliefs. In his writings, the Virginian condemned free society, rejected egalitarian politics, and advocated slavery for all manual workers of whatever color, North as well as South.

Working from the axiom that it is the first "duty of society to protect the weak," Fitzhugh indicted the North for ignoring that responsibility. Its capitalists, he claimed, exploited workers by refusing them a life-sustaining share of what they produced, offering them no guarantee of employment, and abandoning them when ill, injured, or aged. In his judgment, "the profits which capital exacts from labor make free laborers slaves, without the rights, privileges, or advantages of domestic slaves, and capitalists their masters, with all the advantages, and none of the burdens and obligations of the ordinary owners of slaves." Admitting that his assertions currently applied to only a small group of New England factory hands and their employers, Fitzhugh predicted that all Northern workers would become "slaves to capital" once the western territories had been settled.[5]

Drawing upon his reading and a romantically inaccurate view of the Southern plantation as a large, compassionately run multiracial family, Fitzhugh asserted that "public opinion unites with self-interest, domestic affection, and municipal law to protect the slave," its most vulnerable member. Slaves, in contrast to free workers, he wrote, were carefree and happy, in a sense "the freest people in the world. The children and the aged and infirm work not at all, and yet have all the comforts and necessaries of life provided for them." In addition, their wives "do little work, and are protected [by their masters] from the despotism of their husbands. . . . The negro [sic] men and stout boys work, on the average, in good weather, not more than nine hours a day," and, compared with the factory owner, "the master permits the slave to retain a larger [share of] the proceeds of his labor."[6]

Slavery, according to Fitzhugh, also protected the weak in often overlooked ways. Working under the supervision of a capable and compassionate master, the lazy and improvident slaves received protection from the consequences of their shortcomings, and others need not bear the burden of their support. By separating the large masses of the ignorant and morally weak and putting them, in small groups, in daily contact with a master worthy of emulation, plantation slavery reformed them by example. Fitzhugh, though leaving home rarely and making only a single two-month trip to the North, asserted confidently but without foundation that Southern slaveowners everywhere fit the image in his mind.

Although to that point differing little from the rest of slavery's advocates, Fitzhugh boldly took the proslavery argument to its logical conclusion: protecting society's weakest members required that governments first enslave them *legally* and not in the economic manner of Northern factory owners. Taking that step demanded that Fitzhugh put the ax to the tree of American liberty. Rejecting John Locke, Fitzhugh joined Southern elitists in denying that governments drew their powers from the consent of the governed. Even in America, he explained, those who held no property had played little role in the formation of its governments, which he described as "self-elected despotisms" dominated by a "governing class [of] self-elected despots." Though Thomas Jefferson had correctly claimed that men possess natural and inalienable rights that governments must respect, the great Virginian erred in proclaiming the equality of those rights. With all of creation revealing to Fitzhugh the existence of inequality, he leapt to a fantastic conclusion: "About nineteen out of every twenty individuals have [only] a 'natural and inalienable right' to be taken care of and protected, to have guardians, trustees, husbands, or masters; in other words they have a natural and inalienable right to be slaves." Barely "one in twenty" men had the capacity for "command and liberty. Not to make [of] them rulers or masters [would be] as great a violation of natural right as not to make slaves of the mass."[7]

To Fitzhugh's mind the Founders had gotten it all wrong; it "would be far nearer the truth to say, 'that some were born with saddles on their backs, and others booted and spurred to ride them,'—and the riding does them good." The Jeffersonian "doctrine of Human Equality" struck Fitzhugh as nonsense, and the Declaration of Independence and the Virginia Bill of Rights as "absurd and dangerous." In his mind, all of history—and the Bible—supported the notion that slavery was "the natural and normal condition of society." It was, indeed, the basis of all superior civilizations, such as those of ancient Greece and Rome. Free society, not slavery, was "abnormal and anomalous."[8]

Though not widely available in the North, Fitzhugh's writings reached Illinois and Abraham Lincoln, who read the proslavery propagandist's books, articles, and editorials, frequently citing them in his speeches as evidence of the Slave Power's aims. According to historian C. Vann Woodward, Lincoln may even have found in Fitzhugh's *Cannibals All!* or *Sociology for the South* the predictions that contributed to the future president's 1858 "House Divided" prophecy that "this government cannot endure, permanently half *slave* and half *free*. . . . It will become *all* one thing, or *all* the other. Either the *opponents* of slavery, will . . . place it . . . in the course of ultimate extinction; or its *advocates* will put it forward, till it shall become alike lawful in *all* the States, *old* as well as *new*—*North* as well as *South*."[9]

~ Few of slavery's advocates found it politic to go as far as Lincoln feared or Fitzhugh hoped.[10] Still, they were no less committed to it than the reactionary Virginian, and they, too, demanded that, whatever might be done about an institution so deeply embedded in their society, the North and the national government must keep hands off and yield the initiative to the South. Such feelings were at least as old as the Continental Congress, whose leading slaveholders nevertheless regarded slavery as no better than a temporarily necessary evil, one that future generations must eliminate. Responding to such beliefs, states north of Maryland had begun gradually to abolish slavery in the decades after 1776, and Congress soon barred it from the Northwest Territory—the future Midwest—and later banned the import of slaves.

Except for the 1820 compromise over the status of slavery in the Louisiana Purchase, the national debate over slavery subsided until the 1830s. In that decade, as William Lloyd Garrison of Massachusetts began calling slavery a sin and advocated its immediate abolition throughout the United States, a new generation of Southerners turned toward rather than away from the South's peculiar institution. Though Virginia's frightened intellectuals and politicians reconsidered slaveownership after Nat Turner's 1831 slave rebellion shook their state, more and more Southerners began describing slavery as a positive good rather than as a necessary evil. Reporting the Virginia legislature's 1831–32 slavery debate, College of William and Mary professor and slaveowner Thomas Dew advanced a defense that earned him the college's presidency and prompted an outpouring of similar arguments.

A transitional figure, Dew made some use of slavery's traditional defenses: Even if, in the abstract, it might be wrong and un-Christian, Southerners bore no responsibility for bringing Africans to North America. Ignoring the possibility of a biracial society, he maintained that the nation could not now afford to purchase the slaves' freedom and return them to Africa. Continued slavery seemed the only option. Looking on the positive side, Dew then reminded readers that the achievements of ancient Greece and Rome had rested on slavery. Nor could anyone tell Southerners where the Bible condemned it. Contrary to Jefferson's predictions, Dew argued that slave ownership had neither corrupted masters nor made slaves hateful, perhaps because they benefited from close contact with Christian civilization.

Reflecting the racial beliefs of most Americans, both North and South, Dew also denied that large numbers of emancipated slaves might safely remain in the United States. Prone to crime, too lazy to work without close supervision, and intellectually unfit for citizenship, their presence posed a threat of race war should Southern whites and free blacks eventually struggle for dominance. Emancipation risked, therefore, a great deal of harm while doing little to benefit either race.

Following the abolitionists' 1835 use of the postal service to distribute antislavery literature throughout the South, alarmed Southerners censored the mails and pushed beyond hesitant defenses like Dew's. Although never abandoning any useful argument, the defense of bondage came to center on claims that science, history, and religion justified slavery, now described as a positive good—a benefit to both masters and slaves and the proper basis of republican government.

In an 1837 speech before his state's Society for the Advancement of Learning, South Carolina lawyer, judge, and politician William Harper stopped short of Fitzhugh's advocacy of slavery for all manual workers, whatever their color, while offering a comprehensive defense of the South's peculiar institution. Discovering that "domestic slavery exists over the far greater portion of the inhabited earth," Harper concluded that the institution must be "deeply founded in the nature of man and the exigencies of human society." That was so because a man typically "will not labour beyond what is absolutely necessary to maintain his existence." Without the "coercion of Slavery" forming "man to habits of labour," society could not accumulate the wealth needed to advance civilization. Confident of God's civilizing intentions, Harper believed that the "finger of heaven itself" had pointed Southerners to "a race of men . . . already enslaved" in Africa who might help them fulfill "the first great command to subdue and replenish the earth."[11]

Sounding like Fitzhugh and appealing to an elitist form of republicanism, Harper also challenged as "sentimental" and "palpably false" all attacks on slavery based upon the Declaration of Independence. Whatever Jefferson may have written, men were born not free but dependent, and differences in wealth, status, strength, knowledge, and power kept most men less than free and equal. Nor did a man's claim to liberty extend so far as to deny society's right to limit that freedom for a good purpose. Confident of divine intentions, Harper added that it was "the order of nature and of God, that the being of superior faculties and knowledge, and therefore of superior power, should control and dispose of those who are inferior. It is . . . in the order of nature that men should enslave each other."[12] Small wonder that such thinking led many Northerners to regard the Slave Power as a threat to republican institutions and civil rights.

Another Southern intellectual, the Reverend Thornton Stringfellow, a Baptist minister and the owner of a Virginia plantation served by seventy slaves, undertook to counter the abolitionists' charge that slavery was sin. Noah, a man approved by God, had established slavery when he condemned to perpetual servitude the descendants of one of his sons. God, in Stringfellow's opinion, had also endorsed slavery as practiced by Abraham and Isaac and when, through Moses, He gave the Israelites laws on the treatment of slaves. Nor did Jesus ever explicitly condemn slavery, and both Peter and Paul admonished slaves to obey their masters. Surely then, Stringfellow reasoned, slavery violated no Christian principle. To finish his argument with a positive spin, Stringfellow, like Fitzhugh, asserted that the condition of Southern slaves, "*as a class*, is now better than that of any other equal number of laborers on earth, and is daily improving."[13]

Whichever defense of slavery individual Southerners found appealing, some variant of a not always consistent argument remained of paramount importance: a biracial society of equals would destroy the South's way of life and end in utter disaster for both races. Once freed, blacks would become subsistence farmers, causing the collapse of cotton production, the entire Southern economy, and then American commerce. Or, too degraded to manage their own affairs, blacks would turn to crime and, if given political rights, become victims of political demagogues. Worse yet, the two races would mix sexually, to the genetic detriment of superior whites. At that very emotional level, the thought of any disruption of slavery terrified most Southerners, who remained determined that they alone would decide the future of their peculiar institution.

∾ Had the proslavery argument remained a Southern curiosity, it might have alarmed and annoyed few Northerners. In 1857, however, the Supreme Court brought slavery's advocacy fully into national politics and, giving it constitutional sanction, heightened Northern belief in slavery as a threat to its free-labor society. Though such events as the bitter fight over Kansas statehood had already roused the North, the decision of Chief Justice Roger Taney in *Dred Scott v. Sandford** contributed mightily to belief in a Slave Power seeking to legalize slavery throughout the United States.

The case, superbly analyzed by historian Don Fehrenbacher,[14] began on the Mississippi Valley frontier. In 1834, Dr. John Emerson, a Pennsylvanian living in St. Louis, won appointment as an assistant surgeon in the army and took with him to Fort Armstrong in the free state of Illinois his newly purchased slave, Dred Scott. Two years later the army again sent Emerson, with Scott, into free territory when it assigned the doctor to Fort Snelling, which lay in the portion of the 1803 Louisiana Purchase reserved for freedom. While at Snelling, and with Emerson's permission, Scott married another slave—a legal impossibility within the slave

*The Supreme Court report misspelled defendant Sanford's name.

state of Missouri. Though Emerson left the Scotts at Snelling when he returned to St. Louis to wed Eliza Sanford, they joined him in Missouri before all four returned to the fort. Discharged in 1842, Emerson took both his families, slave and free, to Iowa, another free state, and there his wife gave birth to a daughter, Henrietta. By December of the next year Emerson had died, leaving his estate to his wife during her lifetime and naming as executor her brother, John Sanford of St. Louis.

In March 1846, Dred Scott, back again in Missouri, sued Mrs. Emerson for his freedom on the grounds of his four-year residency in a state and a territory from which Congress had barred slavery. Although the Missouri courts had long recognized that masters implicitly emancipated any slave taken to a free area, a state supreme court majority embittered by the Mexican War's revival of the fight over slavery rejected precedent in 1850 and denied Scott his freedom.

By that date Mrs. Emerson had left for Massachusetts, where she soon married Calvin Chaffee, an opponent of slavery, and her brother assumed active management of her affairs. That move allowed Scott's lawyers to change tactics. Because the case now involved residents of different states, the lawyers abandoned plans for an appeal and initiated a new suit in federal court, with John Sanford as defendant. When Scott lost again in the circuit court, his attorneys appealed to the U.S. Supreme Court, which first heard arguments in 1856.

The Court now hearing Scott's appeal had an even more proslavery orientation than its Missouri counterpart. As Andrew Jackson's attorney general, Roger Taney had denied that free blacks had any rights under the Constitution. Appointed to the Court, he used his new position to advance the cause of slavery when he absolved a Maryland slave catcher indicted for kidnapping an alleged fugitive living in Pennsylvania. Believing that the federal government had a constitutional obligation to protect slavery, Chief Justice Taney claimed in another case that Congress had no authority to make prohibition of slavery a condition of statehood, as it had done in the Northwest Ordinance. Presumably, then, the five states of the Midwest might establish the institution, if they so wished. That opinion also implied that states might enslave their free blacks and that the federal government could demand that free states protect ownership of slaves brought within their borders.[15] A proslavery partisan, it seems, led the Court to which Dred Scott appealed his suit for freedom.

Taney's four Southern colleagues gave equally enthusiastic support to slavery. Fehrenbacher described Peter Daniel, the associate justice from Virginia, as a "brooding proslavery fanatic," and James Wayne of Georgia, John Catron of Tennessee, and John Campbell of Alabama as "unreserved defenders of slavery and slaveholding rights in the territories." New York's Samuel Nelson and Pennsylvania's Robert Grier, both doughfaces, or Northern men with Southern principles, reinforced the Court's proslavery Democratic majority. The only justices not in slavery's camp were Benjamin Curtis of Massachusetts, the sole Whig appointed to the Court since 1829, and John McLean of Ohio, a Democrat turned Republican by 1857.[16]

Fehrenbacher found that Scott's suit presented the Court with three questions, not all of which it needed to answer: 1) Could an African American be a citizen, or enough of a citizen to bring suit in a federal court? 2) What was the status of a slave who had returned to a slave state after residing in free territory? 3) And had Congress constitutional authority to prohibit slavery in a territory? With a negative decision on the first one, the Court could have denied jurisdiction and let the Missouri ruling stand. By denying that Scott's residency on free soil made him a free man once back in Missouri, the Court might also have avoided the controversial third question.

For a time, it seemed that the Court would show restraint and do so. After hearing the case argued for a second time in December 1856, only the five Southern justices wished to invalidate the Missouri Compromise—a politically imprudent response to the third question, especially if made by a slim sectional majority. By deciding only the second question, the Court produced a majority of at least six of its seven Democrats and asked Justice Nelson to draft its decision. After finessing the issue of Scott's citizenship, he denied Scott's freedom on the grounds that Dr. Emerson had brought his slave into free territory in response to military orders rather than to a change in residency.

While Nelson wrote, proslavery partisans began to prod the Court's five Southern justices (who needed little encouragement) to strike a blow for the South by including a judgment denying congressional authority to bar slavery in a territory, the third of Fehrenbacher's questions. To his brother Linton, future Confederate vice president Alexander Stephens acknowledged being one of those pressuring the Court, or at least Justice Wayne from his native state of Georgia. President-elect James Buchanan exchanged letters with Tennessee's Justice Catron, with the latter eventually urging Buchanan to persuade fellow Pennsylvanian Grier to support a decision on the territorial issue. Although Republicans shouted conspiracy when the Court rendered its final decision, they did so for the wrong reason. They reacted to a whispered conversation between Taney and Buchanan at the latter's inaugural rather than to knowledge of the influence that had been improperly brought to bear on various members of the Court.

Each member of the Court ultimately wrote his own opinion in the case, though sometimes failing to address each of the questions before the high tribunal. Even so, six of the justices clearly supported invalidation of the Missouri Compromise, and seven held that Scott remained a slave. The opinion of Chief Justice Taney, properly regarded as the decision of the Court, ignited a political firestorm when it invalidated the Missouri Compromise, a long-standing piece of congressional legislation. The bellicose manner in which he expressed the proslavery position only piled up more fuel for the conflagration to come.

In rejecting Scott's claim to citizenship, Taney wrote as though he saw no distinction between free blacks and slaves. Ignoring a mass of contrary evidence and inference, he denied that blacks had been state citizens before 1789 and that states had the power to make them so "within the meaning of the Constitution."[17] Lying outside the compass of the Declaration of Independence and excluded, he falsely claimed, from constitutional protections, blacks could not bring suit in federal courts. With Scott consequently still a slave, Taney might have ended the case there with a minimum of controversy. He nevertheless provoked outrage among abolitionists with the infamous claim that blacks were "beings of an inferior order, and altogether unfit to associate with the white race, either in social or political relations; and so far inferior, that they had no rights which the white man was bound to respect."[18]

Although he intended partly to buttress his rejection of Scott's citizenship but primarily to deny congressional authority over slavery in the territories, Taney alarmed Northerners when he appeared to address the merits of a case that should have been dismissed when the Court declared that Scott lacked standing to sue. Aiming to guard slavery against federal interference while also demanding that the government protect it, Taney produced a tortured argument ignoring the plain language of the Constitution and decades of congressional practice. In so doing, he attempted to smash both the platform of the Republican Party (its determination to bar slavery from the territories) and the doctrine of Popular Sovereignty (with which Northern Democrats hoped to win the 1860 presidential election). Worse yet, Taney asserted that Scott would not have become a free man even if carried into free territory by an owner intending to become a permanent resident. Northerners rightly wondered what that might mean for their ability to exclude slavery from their midst.

Fehrenbacher, who has given the *Dred Scott* case its most definitive treatment, concluded that Taney wrote his opinion with an "emotional commitment so intense that it made perception and logic utterly subservient" to his purposes. His argument constituted an "extraordinary cumulation of error, inconsistency, and misrepresentation, dispensed with . . . pontifical self-assurance." Distorting "law and history . . . to serve a passionate purpose," Taney had sought to give conclusive constitutional protection to "southern life and values, which seemed organically linked to the peculiar institution and unpreservable without it."[19]

Knowing in advance of the Court's decision but speaking as though he did not, Buchanan also sought to undermine Republicans and appease the South by including in his inaugural address an appeal to "all good citizens" to join him in submission to the Court's judgment, "whatever this may be." When announced, the decision found most Democrats happily united in support of it.[20]

With the Court seemingly invalidating the definitive plank of their platform, Republicans had little choice but to protest,

which would open them to politically motivated charges of a trea-
sonous defiance of the nation's highest tribunal. With most Northern states already denying blacks full citizenship, Republicans
had no wish to challenge that part of Taney's opinion. They also
failed to attack the Chief Justice's glaring factual errors and
twisted reasoning; perhaps his shortcomings lay beyond their ken
or, they may have assumed, the public's comprehension. Because
the Court had denied Scott's citizenship and therefore his capacity to sue, most Republicans simply maintained that the Court
lacked jurisdiction to answer the other two questions before it.
The other parts of Taney's opinion therefore constituted *obiter
dicta*—nonbinding passing remarks without legal meaning, observations that one might freely criticize without challenging the
authority of the Court. In that way, most Republicans claimed
that Taney's comments on the status of slaves temporarily on free
soil and the validity of the Missouri Compromise placed no limits on Northern interests or their party's platform.

Although arriving at similar conclusions, Lincoln, in his June
1857 speech in Springfield, Illinois, reached them along a different path, one that ironically reflected Taney's legal reasoning
when the future chief justice was Andrew Jackson's attorney general. All branches of the government, the future president asserted, had a co-equal authority to interpret the Constitution, at
least until a controversial issue had become fully debated and
finally settled by other and unanimous Court decisions not motivated by partisanship. To believe otherwise, Lincoln maintained,
was to advance a claim for judicial supremacy that threatened
popular government.

Republicans joined, however, in expressing fears that the Supreme Court would soon override the rights of free states, forcing them to accept slavery against their will. The undecided
Lemmon case, in which New York had freed a group of slaves tran-
siting through its territory, seemed the likely occasion for another
expansive proslavery decision, a second *Dred Scott*. Already
roused by Southern efforts to force slavery onto unwilling Kansans, outraged Northerners became more receptive to predictions
that the Taney Court would soon deny free states the right to
prohibit slavery within their borders. What had been the "lurid
fantasy of paranoid imaginations" before 1850 had become, wrote

historian William Wiecek, a reasonable fear.[21] There seemed to be no limit to Slave Power aggression.

Even a few Democrats saw no end to it. In a September 1859 *Harper's* article, Senator Stephen Douglas of Illinois, the North's leading Democrat, speculated about the Court's intentions. If the Constitution established slavery in Kansas "or any other Territory beyond the power of the people to control it by law, how can the conclusion be resisted that slavery is essentially established in like manner and by the same authority in all the States of the Union?" Apparently fearful of the Court's reaching just that conclusion, Douglas reasoned that "if it be the imperative duty of Congress to provide by law for the protection of slave property in the Territories," it must also be "the duty of Congress . . . to provide similar protection to slave property in all the States of the Union."[22] Who or what, then, might protect Northerners against a proslavery federal government seemingly at the beck and call of an overbearing Slave Power? By the time of John Brown's raid, residents of both sections, it seemed, believed that they had much to fear from the other.

NOTES

1. Fitzhugh in his *Sociology for the South* (1854) quoted in C. Vann Woodward's introduction, "George Fitzhugh, *Sui Generis*," to Fitzhugh's *Cannibals All! or Slaves without Masters* (1857; reprint ed., Cambridge, MA: Belknap Press of Harvard University Press, 1960), xxx.

2. Taney's opinion in *Dred Scott v. Sandford* quoted in Don E. Fehrenbacher, *Slavery, Law, and Politics: The Dred Scott Case in Historical Perspective* (Oxford: Oxford University Press, 1981), 190.

3. The portions of this chapter on George Fitzhugh are based principally on his *Cannibals All!*; Woodward, "Fitzhugh"; and Fitzhugh's "Southern Thought" reprinted in Drew Gilpin Faust, ed., *The Ideology of Slavery: Proslavery Thought in the Antebellum South, 1830–1860* (Baton Rouge: Louisiana State University Press, 1981), 272–99.

4. A Fitzhugh neighbor quoted in Woodward, "Fitzhugh," xii.

5. Fitzhugh, *Cannibals All!*, 13, and "Southern Thought," 282 and 293.

6. Fitzhugh, *Cannibals All!*, 17–18 and 25.

7. Ibid., 69 and 243.

8. Fitzhugh's *Treatise on Sociology* quoted in Woodward, "Fitzhugh," xix–xx; Fitzhugh, *Cannibals All!*, 40; and Fitzhugh, "Southern Thought," 279.

9. Lincoln, with his emphasis, quoted in David H. Donald, *Lincoln* (London: Jonathan Cape, 1995), 206.

10. Important proslavery writings by Thomas Dew, "Abolition of Negro Slavery," William Harper, "Memoir on Slavery," Thornton Stringfellow, "A Brief Examination of Scripture Testimony on the Institution of Slavery" as described in the following paragraphs are reprinted in Faust, *Ideology of Slavery*, 21–77, 78–135, and 136–67, respectively. For one whose conclusions are as peculiar as those of Fitzhugh see Henry Hughes, the last portion of "Treatise on Sociology" reprinted in ibid., 239–71. On proslavery generally see Larry E. Tise, *Proslavery: A History of the Defense of Slavery in America, 1701–1840* (Athens: University of Georgia Press, 1987), and Paul Finkelman, ed., *Articles on American Slavery*, vol. 12, *Proslavery Thought, Ideology, and Politics* (New York: Garland, 1989).

11. Harper, "Memoir on Slavery," in Faust, *Ideology of Slavery*, 79–81 and 120–21.

12. Ibid., 83 and 89.

13. Stringfellow, "Brief Examination," in ibid., 166.

14. This section on Roger Taney and the *Dred Scott* case is based upon Fehrenbacher, *Slavery, Law, and Politics*.

15. On the significance of Taney's decision regarding the Northwest Ordinance see William M. Wiecek, "Slavery and Abolition before the United States Supreme Court, 1820–1860," *Journal of American History* 65 (June 1978): 53–54.

16. Fehrenbacher, *Slavery, Law, and Politics*, 118–19.

17. Ibid., 189.

18. Ibid., 189–90.

19. Ibid., 288.

20. The Buchanan quotation is from his March 4, 1857, Inaugural Address reprinted in James D. Richardson, ed., *Compilation of the Messages and Papers of the Presidents, 1798–1897*, 10 vols. (Washington, DC: By Authority of Congress, 1899), 5:431.

21. Wiecek, "Slavery and the Court," 55.

22. Douglas quoted in Fehrenbacher, *Slavery, Law, and Politics*, 271–72.

PART TWO

THE SECESSION CAMPAIGN

The successful revolutionary must create
effective organizations and arouse masses.
The secessionists did both.
—Historian William L. Barney*

ONLY RARELY DO violent political upheavals result from a sponta-
neous burst of popular fervor. Most often a relatively few individuals committed to political change set out to create new
attitudes. They undermine the legitimacy of the present government, paint a grand picture of an alternative political order, and
inspire an otherwise apathetic public to action. The secession of
the Deep South offers no exception to that rule, and disunion's
principal advocates have become known to history as fire-
eaters—not a name they usually applied to themselves. As per-
sistent advocates of Southern independence, they took sectional
feeling and an awareness of distinctive Southern interests to a
new stage, one incompatible with loyalty to the United States.
Only within a confederacy of slave states and not by means of
sectional compromise, they believed, could the South secure its
interests against attack by the federal government.

Active in some cases for decades, fire-eaters such as South
Carolina's Barnwell Rhett, Alabama's William Yancey, Virginia's
Beverley Tucker and Edmund Ruffin, and Mississippi's John
Quitman did an insurgent's work. They spelled out the horrors
that would accompany a feared emancipation of the South's human property and argued that only independence could secure
slavery, Southern liberties, and the South's way of life. To achieve

*William L. Barney, *The Secessionist Impulse: Alabama and Mississippi
in 1860* (Princeton, NJ: Princeton University Press, 1974), 230.

their goal, the fire-eaters rejected Stephen Douglas of Illinois, the nation's leading Democratic politician, and fractured his party, even though it had long enabled the South to dominate national politics. For the 1860 presidential contest, they created a Southern sectional party led by Vice President John Breckinridge, knowing full well that his candidacy would most likely ensure Republican victory, which many had made the justification for secession. With Abraham Lincoln the winner in the presidential election, the surge in Southern support for disunion threw conservatives such as Georgia's Alexander Stephens on the defensive and gave victory to secession's advocates in the seven states of the Deep South. By the time their representatives gathered in Montgomery, Alabama, to form a new government, leadership had returned to more moderate hands, bringing to the fore men such as Mississippi's Jefferson Davis.

CHAPTER THREE

BARNWELL RHETT,
THE FIRE-EATERS, AND
SOUTHERN INDEPENDENCE

I will test, for myself and for my children,
whether South Carolina is a State or an humbled
and degraded province, existing only at the mercy
of an unscrupulous and fanatical tyranny.
—Barnwell Rhett[1]

THOUGH BARNWELL RHETT, the Father of Secession, ultimately owned several plantations, he had not been born to great wealth. Taught to read by his grandmother, he left Beaufort College at seventeen to help his father manage the family's South Carolina plantation. At nineteen he became free to study law in Charleston under Thomas Grimké, brother of the two subsequently famous abolitionist sisters. How ironic that secession's best-known agitator had studied law with a leader of South Carolina's antislavery American Colonization Society!

Admitted to the bar two years later, Rhett practiced in Beaufort until 1823, when he was invited to become the law partner of his better-known cousin, Robert Barnwell. Intending a career in politics, the young lawyer, born Robert Barnwell Smith, soon thereafter adopted the surname of a distinguished ancestor and ignored his commonplace first name. In aristocratic South Carolina, Robert Smith could not match the cachet of Barnwell Rhett.

Impressed with Rhett's legal skills and oratory, his neighbors sent him to the South Carolina legislature in 1826, just in time for the tariff controversy that ended in nullification and Rhett's inclusion in John Calhoun's circle. As a youthful legislator in 1828, he had warned his constituents that a protective tariff robbed them of their property, and two years later, at a state's rights meeting, he openly embraced disunion as the best response to unconstitutional legislation. Even as the nullification crisis drew to a compromised close in 1833, Rhett advocated disunion, describing a "Confederacy of the Southern States . . . [as] a happy termination—happy beyond expectation, of our long struggle for our rights against oppression."[2] He had come early to secession's cause, and he would stay the course.

A decade later, when Calhoun temporized in hopes of gaining the presidency, Rhett briefly broke with his mentor and at Bluffton urged South Carolinians to act alone in pursuit of their independence. Though both men threatened disunion, Calhoun did so in the expectation that such action would force the North to moderate its demands and thereby preserve the Union. He sought, not independence, but compromise on Southern terms.

In that outcome, Rhett had little interest. For political parties as a means to achieve compromise, he had even less regard. In his opinion, parties were dangerous alliances with Northern politicians, and pursuing Southern interests through intraparty compromises allowed outsiders to meddle with slavery—never a safe policy for a community such as South Carolina's, in which whites were only two-fifths of the population. Rather than accept any limitations on their rights, Rhett wanted South Carolinians—and, indeed, all Southerners—to unite across party lines and unyieldingly defend slavery and Southern interests as he defined them.

In addition to a lack of faith in Calhoun's strategy and the Democratic Party, Rhett rejected conventions of slave states as a means to disrupt the Union. Joint action, he believed, must always end in failure because a few states would inevitably favor compromise, which to Rhett meant submission to federal assaults on the South's constitutional rights. Rather than attempt to influence federal policy, secession must aim at a Southern confederacy achieved through separate state action. Professing little fear of such "Revolution!" Rhett warned South Carolinians in 1850 that if they refused to resist federal usurpation, they must ultimately face "one evil, worse, far worse in its existence and consequences, than Revolution—Slavery."[3] Strong language perhaps, but in his view any loss of control over property constituted slavery, even it did not put masters in the field and under the lash.

Believing that an antislavery North would never respect Southern rights, Rhett, both in season and out, argued for the formation of a Southern confederacy. Beyond the reach of abolitionist conspirators, and with Southern forces patrolling their Northern border, the slave states might expand into New Mexico and Utah, drawing into their orbit free California and creating an imperial slave republic as they absorbed Cuba, all of Mexico, and northern South America. Railroad construction would boom, promoting economic development. With its trade freed of protective tariffs, the new slave nation would enjoy an immense increase in European commerce and investment and achieve unrivaled industrial and agricultural progress. In a revised version of the American mission, a Southern confederacy would also demonstrate to the world the superiority of a slaveholding republic. Nor was it a small matter that secession would substitute for the dishonorable compromises of the past a bold defense of Southern liberties.

Though never wavering in his goals, Rhett did sometimes modify his tactics. In 1850, for example, he supported Mississippi's call for a slave-state convention at Nashville, where a united South might warn Congress against barring its peculiar institution from the territory won in the 1846 war with Mexico. When the convention suggested compromise—dividing the Mexican Cession between slave and free areas—it confirmed Rhett's worst fears. In his speech closing the convention, he charged that Southern forbearance would feed the North's "lust of power" and its determination to "assail and destroy slavery in the South." The slave states, he predicted, "must rule themselves or perish."[4]

Giving the back of its hand to Nashville, Congress admitted California directly into the Union as a free state, which upset the sectional balance in the Senate. Taking no position on the status of slavery elsewhere in the Mexican Cession, Congress implicitly applied to the region the principle of Popular Sovereignty, meaning that its residents might themselves decide (at some time left purposely vague) whether to accept or reject slavery.

When that compromise, for a while, helped unionists gain the upper hand throughout the South, Rhett realized that inflammatory language and advocacy of separate state action held little appeal for the moment, and he retired from active politics.

Remaining committed to secession, however, he gained new popularity following the Republican Party's surprising demonstration of strength in the 1856 presidential election. Assuming full ownership of the Charleston *Mercury* the next year, Rhett and his son repeatedly told Southerners that their section had become a helpless minority ruled by the antislavery North.

Having in advance of John Brown's raid predicted that abolitionists would soon invade the South to promote servile insurrection, Rhett appeared a prophet in October 1859, and he soon joined the drive to either rule or ruin the 1860 Democratic convention scheduled for Charleston. If the party and its nominee refused to accept the extension of slavery and a federal slave code for the territories, Rhett would help destroy it, thereby paving the way for a Republican victory in November. That surely would prompt secession.

South Carolina unionist Benjamin Perry's characterization of radical secessionists as "young enthusiasts inspired with notions of personal honor to be defended and individual glory, fame and military laurels to be acquired" did not entirely fit the middle-aged Rhett.[5] In regard to two other fire-eaters, however, Perry's shot fell close to the mark. In the 1850s the young men, both grown to adulthood in a political environment superheated by debates over nullification and slavery, eagerly embraced Rhett's dream of a Southern confederacy.

Born in 1824 to a wealthy planter family in the Orangeburg District of the state's midlands, the first of them, Lawrence Keitt, graduated from South Carolina College, studied law, and practiced briefly in his home district. In 1846, when Pennsylvania congressman David Wilmot proposed legislation prohibiting slavery in any lands acquired from Mexico, Keitt's interest turned toward politics. Two years later his neighbors sent him to their state's legislature for the first of three terms, near the end of which the secession-minded Keitt won a special congressional election for Barnwell Rhett's old seat.

William Porcher Miles took a different route to Congress and Southern nationalism. Born in 1822 in Rhett's coastal Colleton District, he also received a private education (at Calhoun's old school) before attending the College of Charleston, where he befriended James D. B. De Bow, another future fire-eater. The scholarly Miles also began the study of law but quickly abandoned it to become a professor of mathmatics at his alma mater. Though the Wilmot Proviso had provoked him as well, Miles limited his protests to speaking and writing. He sought political office only in 1855, as mayor of Charleston, but won a seat in Congress in 1856, the year in which Republicans exacerbated Southern fears and hostility by the near success of John Frémont as their first presidential candidate.

Having much in common, Keitt and Miles possessed quite different temperaments. The arrogant Keitt's hot temper and rash manner, regarded as knightly in the antebellum South, easily matched the violence of his secessionist language. Twice physically prevented from brawling on the floor of the House, he faced no restraint when accompanying South Carolina hothead Preston Brooks to the Senate chamber in late May 1857. They found Charles Sumner, the Republican senator from Massachusetts, seated at his desk, and Brooks proceeded to beat the older man insensible as punishment for an antislavery speech, "The Crime against Kansas," in which Sumner had maligned Brooks's senatorial cousin. While Representative Brooks wielded his cane, Keitt brandished his to keep others from coming to the aid of the fallen Republican. Facing expulsion and censure for what they considered a chivalric act, Brooks and Keitt resigned. When constituents sent Brooks new canes and promptly reelected both men to Congress, many in the North found confirmation of slavery's brutalizing effects, even on masters.

After taking his seat in Congress, the even-tempered Miles fell under the influence of Keitt, publisher James De Bow, writer William Gilmore Simms, and historian William Trescott, radicals all. Guided by them, he abandoned his early support for cooperative secession, one achieved jointly with other slave states, and soon spoke out for immediate and separate state action. He also jettisoned his abstract speeches and his respect for the rules of the House in favor of language that could "revolutionize a nation." Though avoiding physical assaults in the manner of Keitt, by late 1858 Miles was ready to "fight it out" in Congress and, like other fire-eaters, to prepare "the Southern mind for a war to the knife."[6]

Validating Perry's observation about the typical fire-eater's emphasis on honor, Miles considered Northern criticism of slavery and opposition to its extension an attack on his character. Northerners spoke, he claimed, as though Southerners "must be fumigated and purified from every Southern taint—must pass through a sort of moral quarantine, before . . . [being] allowed to enter the precincts of the free-soil paradise!" To Miles, any insulting compromise on slavery's access to the territories would brand Southerners as inferior, marking them as people of "perverse moral obliquity . . . not entitled to the enjoyment of full participation in the common goods and property of the Republic." Refusing submission to "such a monstrous injustice," Miles called upon Carolinians to emulate their Revolutionary fathers and struggle against the North's attempt to place upon them the "seal of inferiority." Should they hold back, putting "dollars and cents" ahead of principle, Carolinians would prove themselves unworthy, even degenerate.[7]

Defense of his and the South's honor equally motivated Keitt and explains his support for Brooks's brutal caning of Sumner and his resignation when the House censured him for his role in the assault. Believing that "no people degraded can [long remain] free," Keitt called upon Southerners to resist "stigmatizing" limits on slavery's expansion. Those who yielded acted in a "base" and "craven" manner, encouraging abolitionist attempts to "overthrow [the South's] honor, peace, and existence." Rather than submit, equivalent to making "us change places with our slaves," Keitt "would shatter this Republic from turret to foundation stone."[8]

~~ Antebellum Southerners had no need to journey to South Carolina or the District of Columbia to hear such language. Across the Deep South, fire-eaters labored to convince their fellow citizens that the North threatened a way of life that only a slave republic might secure. For several of the most prominent radicals, however, South Carolina had served as nursery and training school.

Louis Wigfall, born in 1816 to plantation wealth in western South Carolina, shared much with Miles and Keitt—private education, graduation from a South Carolina college, the early pursuit of a legal career, a youthful commitment to secession, an exaggerated sense of honor, and, like Keitt, a love of violence almost for its own sake. Wigfall's other enthusiasms—wine, women, and gambling—soon put him deeply in debt, and his loose tongue led to several fights and duels. Having lost property, home, slaves, livestock, books, and much of his reputation, he escaped to Texas in 1846. His secessionist views, advocacy of slavery's extension, and attacks on Sam Houston as prone to compromise soon won him a seat in his new state's legislature and the publication of his writings in *De Bow's Review*. Following John Brown's raid on Harpers Ferry, Wigfall became a candidate for a seat in the U.S. Senate, which he won in December 1859. From that stage he vigorously defended the South's honor and launched attacks against the North with language similar to Rhett's. To Northern senators, he complained: "You . . . degrade us, deride us, tell us we shall live under a Government that we say is not tasteful to us; you tell us that we are degraded, that we are not your equals." Before remaining in such a Union, Wigfall would "burst it; . . . fracture it, splinter it into more fragments than gunpowder would blow glass."[9]

Another South Carolina-born radical, James De Bow, defied fire-eater custom, neither romanticizing the South nor engaging in verbal pyrotechnics. Born in 1820 to an impoverished Charleston merchant who met an early death, De Bow in his teens helped support the family by working as a wholesale grocery clerk. Educating himself, he obtained a teaching position and studied agriculture at a vocational institute. After saving enough money, he enrolled at the College of Charleston, where he met Miles. Upon graduation, De Bow, too, read law for a year and passed the bar examination; but, bored by the thought of a legal career, he decided to make his way as a writer. As a contributor and then junior editor of the *Southern Quarterly Review*, he subsisted on literature while studying trade and statistics, which convinced him that the South needed a commercial journal to promote its economic development. In pursuit of that goal, he left Charleston for New Orleans in 1845 and there founded the review eventually bearing his name and enabling him to reach a wider audience than did most fire-eaters.[10]

Like them, De Bow linked his Southern nationalism with the usual proslavery arguments, though often giving them a commercial twist. Slavery, he wrote, rather than being a drag on the Southern economy, was the key to the region's economic revival as well as to American prosperity: "Civilization itself may almost be said to depend upon the continual servitude of the blacks in America."[11] To that end, De Bow joined Rhett and others in believing that slavery must expand into the American West and ultimately to Mexico and Central America, which he thought justified reopening the African slave trade.

Though he would tolerate no outside interference with slavery, De Bow unromantically exhorted Southerners to relinquish their backward-looking ways and tendency to blame every problem on the North. Whether or not it seceded, the South must build mills and railroads, either achieving true equality by matching the North's economic position within the Union or becoming strong enough to prosper and defend itself outside it. To safeguard their proper place, Southerners must also educate themselves; raw physical courage guaranteed success neither in commercial competition nor on the field of battle.

As professor of commerce at the University of Louisiana by 1849 and director of the U.S. Bureau of the Census in the Pierce administration, De Bow continued to emphasize his rational side. He proclaimed both his affection for the Union and his hope that the South would grow to hold a commercially distinguished place within it. Holding a federal position and relying upon Southern moderates to buy his *Review* account for De Bow's restraint, even as the Compromise of 1850 converted him to a fully radical position on secession.

When his or the South's honor seemed at stake, moreover, De Bow could become as emotionally heated as Keitt or Wigfall: "As Southerners, as *Americans*, as MEN, we deny the right of being *called to account* for our institutions, our policy, our laws, or our government." Slavery represented "country, life, death—everything." With the rise of the Republican Party and the eventual rejection of slavery in Kansas, De Bow regularly expressed the opinion that secession had become inevitable, the only "above board and manly" course.[12] Committed to Southern independence, he abandoned his earlier analyses to argue that the economic power of cotton alone would enable a slave confederacy to succeed without prior industrial and commercial development.

〜 Though it might seem that something in the soil or air of South Carolina spawned fire-eaters, that is a too-hasty conclusion. Nor did all leading fire-eaters reside in the Deep South. Beverley Tucker, the oldest of the well-known Southern nationalists, was born in 1784 into a prominent Virginia family. Following graduation from the College of William and Mary, a failed legal practice, and undistinguished service in the War of 1812, Tucker headed for the Missouri Territory, where his education and social skills helped him become a successful lawyer and farmer.

When New York's James Talmadge attempted to add to the Missouri statehood bill an amendment calling for the gradual elimination of slavery, Tucker rushed to defend the South's peculiar institution. Yielding to Northern dictation, he warned, would reduce Missourians to "the veriest political slaves, divested of the only right which gives . . . citizenship—the right of governing themselves." If Congress had authority to make such demands on a future state, it might even make citizens, legislators, and judges of former slaves. When Missourians accepted the subsequent compromise, which enabled them to retain slavery but divided the remainder of the Louisiana Purchase between slave and free along a line extending westward from the state's southern border, their lack of principle disgusted Tucker. "I vowed then," he recalled in 1851, the year of his death, "and have repeated the vow, *de diem in diem*, that I will never give rest to my eyes nor slumber to my eyelids until [the Union] is shattered into pieces."[13] One need not be young, a South Carolinian, or anticipating a Republican presidency to become a fire-eater.

Even so, Tucker remained in Missouri for another dozen years before leaving for Virginia and, soon thereafter, the William and Mary Chair of Law, a position once held by his antislavery father. So situated, the younger Tucker began his life's work as a proslavery propagandist of secession, which his studies of sovereignty indicated was a more constitutionally sound response to protective tariffs than nullification. He schooled his students to be ever vigilant, opposing even minor increases in federal power because they led inevitably to further usurpation, such as congressional attempts to limit the extension of slavery into the territories. The South's lack of virtue, as demonstrated by its devotion to political parties and respect for politicians who pandered to the masses, equally alarmed the elitist Tucker, who, like the principal fire-eaters, rejected Jefferson's views on human rights. Rejecting also his father's condemnation of slavery, Tucker indoctrinated his students in the belief that the inherent racial inferiority of blacks made them suitable subjects for slavery, an institution he regarded as essential to republican government. That being so, the abolitionists must be silenced.

Not all of Tucker's "pupils" attended William and Mary. His support for South Carolina politician James Hammond led to friendship, and the latter drew into their alliance William Gilmore Simms, who helped Tucker publish many of his essays. To print his secessionist novel, *The Partisan Leader*, Tucker turned to Duff Green, newspaperman and Calhoun supporter. To Southern men of affairs, Tucker advised watchfulness: wait for an opening, for some event that would enable them to strike for independence. Despite his hopes, the Compromise of 1850 failed to provide the occasion, and Tucker died the next year without ever seeing the slave confederacy for which he longed and labored.

Still, his arguments survived. In an 1848 Senate speech, Hammond revealed Tucker's influence when asserting that "Cotton is King." The professor's lectures on sovereignty, his justification of secession, and his determination to defend slavery and Southern independence had reached a wide audience. According to Tucker's biographer, it included a number of men who "figured prominently in the secession of Virginia, no doubt partly because of the impact he had on them."[14]

Another Virginian of Tucker's generation arrived at secession in the manner of the younger De Bow, through study of the Southern economy. Scion of a Virginia family with seventeenth-century roots and of a father with several plantations and well over one hundred slaves, Edmund Ruffin, wrote historian Eric Walther, became the "most fanatic fire-eater of all" and, in the opinion of his biographer, the very "symbol of secession and the Old South." In his sixties, Ruffin even donned a cadet's uniform in order to march with the Virginia Military Institute's cadets to observe John Brown's hanging. To be on hand for the attack on Fort Sumter, he joined South Carolina's Palmetto Guard and helped initiate the assault by firing one of its first cannon shots. Unable to accept defeat, he took his life in June 1865. First, however, Ruffin became an agricultural reformer.[15]

Alcohol, a young woman, and the inheritance of a plantation and slaves drew Ruffin from his studies at the College of William and Mary, which suspended him on the eve of the War of 1812. After serving in the war, he began to realize the extent to which decades of growing tobacco had robbed his plantation of its fertility. Now he turned to the books in earnest. When crop rotation and generous applications of animal manure and vegetable compost produced only temporary increases in yield, he read further, discovering that reducing the acidity of the soil through application of lime might increase the effectiveness of his natural fertilizers. Heavy doses of the lime-rich fossil shells plentiful in his part of Virginia soon helped Ruffin and his slaves increase the plantation's grain crop by 40 percent. Having found the key to agricultural plenty, Ruffin expected his fellow planters to adopt his methods, which he promulgated in speeches, articles, essays, and the agricultural journal that he founded to publicize his theories. To his chagrin, Virginia's planters ignored him.

Meanwhile, Ruffin's interest in secession slowly developed. Once a Jeffersonian Republican of the old school, he regarded even the moderately protective Tariff of 1816 as an abuse of federal power, and by the 1840s he concluded that the national government had become unconstitutionally strengthened without ever violating the letter of its founding document. Even so, Ruffin found Virginians as slow to awake to political danger as they had been to agricultural decline. Being again ignored fed the bitterness of a man who craved public adulation.

After studying the proslavery opinions of Thomas Dew, Ruffin abandoned his earlier opinion that slavery was an evil. His agricultural work having brought him into contact with James Hammond, Ruffin also accepted the argument of the South Carolinian's Clarkson letters, which proclaimed the superiority of slave society. The Compromise of 1850 then made Ruffin a secessionist. He promptly threw himself into his new cause, replacing his formerly scholarly approach to issues with a fire-eater's polemical and emotional style. "I will not pretend," he now announced, "to restrain my pen, nor attempt to be correct in plan or expression—as is more or less usually the case in my writing."[16]

In the articles and one novel that flowed from his pen, Ruffin argued the constitutionality of secession and asserted that abolitionists aimed to limit slavery's spread and then destroy the institution on which the South depended. Only secession, which he believed would not end in war, could secure to planters their property and preserve the slaves essential to the South's agricultural revival. With letters, articles, speeches, and travels, Ruffin widened his circle of secessionist acquaintances, including not only Hammond and Tucker but also Rhett, De Bow, and Keitt. Once De Bow had demonstrated how the South's annual commercial conventions might be politicized as a means to promote secession, Ruffin enthusiastically used them in his propaganda campaign. Hoping to aid his cause by drawing attention to himself, Ruffin dressed in a plain Virginia-made suit (no Northern imports for him) and on public occasions carried one of John Brown's pikes as a shocking reminder of what one abolitionist had had in mind for the South. Despite those efforts, according to his biographer, Ruffin "did not become a crucial political figure in the maneuvers that led Virginia or any other state to secede. . . . His speeches and writings were significant, not as statements of a powerful politician, but as expressions of a significant Southern thinker's case for secession."[17]

If all fire-eaters were neither South Carolinians nor young, neither were they all Southern-born. John Quitman, a native of Rhinebeck, New York, migrated by way of Ohio to Natchez, Mississippi, at age twenty-two and there, according to Eric Walther, he became for a time the "most prominent secessionist outside South Carolina."[18] The son of a Lutheran minister, Quitman studied for a single year at Hartwick Academy and taught for another at Mount Airy College before heading west to seek his fortune in Chillicothe, Ohio, where he read for and passed the bar examination in 1821. A chance acquaintance drew him to Mississippi in search of better prospects. Within five years the ambitious New Yorker had joined a successful law practice, married into a wealthy family, and bought a $12,000 plantation and slaves.

As a State's Rights Whig, he supported nullification and became a follower of Calhoun, even as he held a fire-eater's belief in state sovereignty and secession's legality. By 1850, Quitman had served in both houses of the state legislature, commanded a brigade in the Mexican War battle of Monterrey, and as a major general led the assault on Mexico City. Having also acquired five plantations and over four hundred slaves, Quitman became thoroughly proslavery and deeply committed to the Southern way of life, which he believed growing federal power now put at risk.

Elected to Mississippi's governorship at the height of the debate over slavery's status in the Mexican Cession, Quitman prepared for secession by urging the creation of Southern Rights associations in each of his state's counties and inviting the slave states to send delegates to what became the Nashville Convention. When Congress admitted California as a free state, he called his legislature into special session to consider secession, and he extended his earlier plotting with South Carolina governor Whitemarsh Seabrook, who with Quitman sought to lead both states out of the Union. Their scheme collapsed when the Nashville Convention came to naught, and Quitman resigned his office to defend a charge that his support for an expedition to seize Cuba had violated U.S. neutrality laws. Defeated for reelection by the unionist resurgence of 1851, Quitman tried unsuccessfully to launch another Cuba filibustering expedition and in 1855 won election to Congress. Shortly after being reelected in 1857, he ate some contaminated food and died in July 1858, having done, his biographer wrote, "more than any other public man to familiarize Mississippi voters with the states' rights constitutional theories and the secession option."[19]

≈ The fire-eaters would do for the South what Quitman had begun in his adopted state. They accepted and helped to spread the proslavery argument that the South's peculiar institution was no evil but rather a positive good—a benefit to master and slave alike, the basis of a superior civilization, and the only solid foundation for a republic. Struggling to limit the power of the federal government as it bore down on slavery, they called alarmed attention to Washington's and the Northern states' alleged violations of the Constitution—protective tariffs, congressional discussion of slavery, limits on its expansion, and a reluctance to return runaway slaves. With little regard for the rights of other states or their citizens, fire-eaters condemned the North for failing to silence slavery's opponents and limit their activities. After 1856 they frightened the South by predicting that a Republican president would fill patronage offices with abolitionists and make federal garrisons safe havens for escaped slaves. A Republican Congress might, moreover, abolish slavery in the District of Columbia, prohibit the interstate slave trade, and in the future admit none but free states. To hasten creation of a three-quarters antislavery majority, enough to amend the Constitution, Republican state legislatures might even consent to the division of enough of the older states to bring slavery to an end throughout the nation. Emancipation, the fire-eaters declared, would lead to racial amalgamation, white degradation, domination by blacks, and racial conflict—a prediction designed to strike fear even in the hearts of those Southerners who owned no slaves.

To convince Southerners that only secession and a slave confederacy could overcome the Northern threat to the South's way of life, the fire-eaters relied upon books, journals, newspapers, correspondence, and word of mouth to reach educated audiences. Awakening the masses required speeches, their own and those of as many politicians and preachers as could be won to accept their dire prophecies. To one and all they affirmed that Southern independence would bring prosperity by eliminating protective tariffs and ending the South's dependence upon Northern industry. An American slave republic, fire-eaters predicted, would become a great empire as it expanded not only into the West but also southward to Cuba, Mexico, and South America, providing farms and slaves for all white men who desired them. To satisfy prideful Southerners, secession would also restore the South's honor and remove from the section the badge of inferiority and shame imposed upon it by Northern criticism.

Turning arguments, however appealing, into action proved difficult for the fire-eaters, in large part because of their diversity of background and temperament. Quitman, De Bow, and Rhett were self-made men; Keitt, Miles, and Ruffin had been born to wealth. So had Wigfall and Tucker, but they had lost it, at least for a time. Most were agriculturists, but Rhett, Tucker, and De Bow pursued urban occupations, and Ruffin eventually abandoned planting for writing. From their youth, De Bow and Ruffin had tried to improve the South economically, and Miles, Quitman, and Keitt had favored political change. At the same time, most were backward-looking, advocating eighteenth-century elitist republicanism in the age of Jacksonian democracy. Though De Bow and Ruffin had the ability to present reasonable, even scholarly, analyses, they readily yielded to emotion and intemperate language. Wigfall seemed capable of little but insult and abuse in defense of the South. Although such differences enabled them collectively to reach a variety of Southerners, the fire-eaters' arrogance, hypersensitivity, and inflexibility made even limited cooperation extremely difficult, and they established no lasting regional organization or party to promote their ideology and program.

By 1860 the South's fire-eaters had nevertheless conditioned the Southern mind to love slavery, fear the North, suspect the federal government, contemplate secession, and anticipate a glorious future within an imperial slave republic. Lacking a regional organization, they hoped to overcome apathy, crystallize opinion, and turn thought to action by means of an event that would impel the South to strike boldly for independence. The fire-eaters' best orator, William Yancey, would seek to do just that as he set out in 1860 to destroy both the Democratic Party and Stephen Douglas, its leading politician.   '

NOTES

1. Rhett quoted in Eric H. Walther, *The Fire-Eaters* (Baton Rouge: Louisiana State University Press, 1992), 145.

2. This and the paragraphs that follow concerning Barnwell Rhett are based upon Walther, *Fire-Eaters*, 121–59. Rhett is quoted on page 125. See also Laura A. White, *Robert Barnwell Rhett: Father of Secession* (New York: Century, 1931; reprint, 1965).

3. Rhett quoted in Walther, *Fire-Eaters*, 124. John McCardell, *The Idea of a Southern Nation: Southern Nationalists and Southern Nationalism, 1830–1860* (New York: W. W. Norton, 1979), 5–7 and 35–40, distinguishes between sectionalists such as Calhoun and nationalists such as Rhett.

4. Rhett quoted in Walther, *Fire-Eaters*, 138–39.

5. Perry quoted in John Barnwell, *Love of Order: South Carolina's First Secession Crisis* (Chapel Hill: University of North Carolina Press, 1982), 150. The summary of the careers of Keitt and Miles in this and subsequent paragraphs derives from Walther, *Fire-Eaters*, 160–94 and 270–96.

6. Trescott to Miles, May 2, 1858, and Miles to James Hammond, November 10 and 15, 1858, quoted in Walther, *Fire-Eaters*, 284.

7. Miles quoted in ibid., 274–75.

8. Keitt quoted in ibid., 178–79.

9. On Wigfall's career see ibid., 160–94; quoted on 179–80.

10. Information on De Bow in this and subsequent paragraphs is found in ibid., 195–227.

11. De Bow quoted in ibid., 201–2.

12. De Bow quoted in ibid., 211 and 217.

13. Tucker quoted in ibid., 16–17, and David S. Heidler, *Pulling the Temple Down: The Fire-Eaters and the Destruction of the Union* (Mechanicsburg, PA: Stackpole Books, 1994), 42. The summary of Tucker's career in these paragraphs is from Walther, *Fire-Eaters*, 8–47.

14. Robert J. Brugger, *Beverley Tucker: Heart over Head in the Old South* (Baltimore: Johns Hopkins University Press, 1978), xiv.

15. Walther, *Fire-Eaters*, 228, and David F. Allmendinger, Jr., *Ruffin: Family and Reform in the Old South* (New York: Oxford University Press, 1990), 135. The paragraphs on Edmund Ruffin that follow are based upon Walther, *Fire-Eaters*, 228–69. See also Betty L. Mitchell, *Edmund Ruffin: A Biography* (Bloomington: Indiana University Press, 1981).

16. Ruffin quoted in Allmendinger, *Ruffin*, 125.

17. Ibid., 136.

18. Walther, *Fire-Eaters*, 99. The following description of Quitman's role is based upon ibid., 83–111, and Robert E. May, *John A. Quitman: Old South Crusader* (Baton Rouge: Louisiana State University Press, 1985).

19. May, *Quitman*, 351.

CHAPTER FOUR

STEPHEN DOUGLAS, WILLIAM YANCEY, AND THE COLLAPSE OF THE DEMOCRATIC PARTY

The last party, pretending to be a national party,
is broken up, and the antagonism of the two
sections of the Union has nothing to arrest
its fierce collisions.
—Charleston *Mercury*[1]

UNTIL THE LATE 1850S, Stephen Douglas seemed an unlikely target for Southern wrath, even if his origins suggested otherwise.[2] A sixth-generation New Englander of Puritan stock, Douglas seemed destined to become a Whig, and his youthful residence in Canandaigua, New York, a district repeatedly "burned over" by religious revivals, led many youngsters there to evangelical Christianity and abolitionism. Resisting cultural influences, Douglas showed no interest in religion and while a teenager committed himself to the egalitarian political ideals of President Andrew Jackson.

Seeking a legal and political career, Douglas headed west when barely twenty, settling in 1833 in central Illinois, where the state's early immigrants from the South blended with more recent arrivals from the Northeast. Admitted to the bar the next year, Douglas initially had few clients but ample time for his principal interest—politics. Presenting a vigorous defense of Jackson's veto of the bill to recharter the Bank of the United States, Douglas made his political debut and, for his small stature but outsized oratory, soon became known as the Little Giant. For his efforts on behalf of the Democratic Party, the legislature made him a district attorney.

Thus launched, Douglas's political career moved rapidly ahead. In 1836 he won election to the state legislature and, the next year, appointment as registrar of the federal land office in Springfield. After serving as the Illinois secretary of state in 1840, Douglas was appointed to the state supreme court. As judge of the circuit seated at Quincy, he first officially dealt with slavery. In a decision later disputed by Salmon Chase before the U.S. Supreme Court, Douglas upheld the Illinois fugitive slave law and fined a local abolitionist $400 for assisting a runaway.

Before leaving Springfield, however, Douglas suffered a rare setback, one in which Abraham Lincoln played a role. In the 1838 congressional elections, Whig John Todd Stuart, Lincoln's law partner, narrowly defeated Douglas, who during the campaign had held his first debate with Lincoln. Not always opposed, the two young attorneys had ridden the judicial circuit together and once served as co-counsel in a murder case. While in Springfield, Douglas also became closely acquainted with Mary Todd, the future Mrs. Lincoln. A young man in a hurry, Douglas had no time for romance. After two years on the state supreme court, he made another, and successful, run for Congress. Elected to the House again in 1844 and to the Senate three times beginning in 1846, Douglas, except for brief visits to his new home in Chicago, resided in the nation's capital until his death in 1861.

While in Congress, Douglas, a westerner with a national outlook and Southern sympathies, advocated popular democracy, state's rights, and strict constitutional limits on federal power. He further pleased the South by denouncing abolitionism and denying that Congress had authority to abolish slavery. Southerners also liked his opposition to protective tariffs, national banking, and expansive use of federal power, though not his support for congressionally financed improvements in the transportation systems upon which the West depended. They should also have taken comfort from Douglas's 1847 marriage into North Carolina's prominent slaveholding Martin family and later control of his wife's inheritance—a twenty-five-hundred-acre Mississippi cotton plantation and more than one hundred slaves—which Douglas held in trust for their two sons following her death.

A thoroughgoing expansionist, the Little Giant believed that America's destiny lay in the West, to which the nation must extend its democratic institutions. Doing so depended upon maintaining the Union, which he, like free-labor Republicans, considered the guarantee of prosperity and representative government. Douglas consequently sought positions on the House and, later, Senate Committee on Territories, where he pressed for the national domain's rapid organization. Reflecting his faith in the people, he favored putting into the hands of residents all possible control over their local affairs until they achieved an early statehood.

Regarding the South's peculiar institution as "a curse beyond computation, to both black and white," Douglas held Jeffersonian views characteristic of an earlier generation of Southerners. As a public man, however, he derived his position on slavery largely from his belief in black inferiority, faith in popular government, and hopes for the Democratic Party and the Union. Slavery, he thought, should remain a local issue, settled by the residents of states and territories without federal interference. Because national agitation of the issue threatened the unity of both party and nation, Douglas attacked sectionalism in all its guises, from abolitionist demands that Congress end slavery in the District of Columbia to the Southern radicals' insistence that the government protect slavery in the territories. Indifferent to the plight of slaves, Douglas wanted the whole controversy put to rest; the "integrity of this political Union," he judged, was "worth more to humanity than the whole black race."[3]

Attempting to resolve the territorial conflict over slavery in a way compatible with his faith in the people, Douglas made his own the doctrine soon known as Popular Sovereignty. In the opinion of the Little Giant, neither section had any rights in a territory "so far as the institution of slavery is concerned."[4] Only its residents, like those of a state, could determine whether to authorize or exclude the institution. That doctrine seemed to have important political advantages: it might keep the debate over territorial slavery out of Congress, neither impugning Southern honor nor frustrating Northern hopes that climate, geography, and residents migrating to the territories from the more populous North would claim them for free soil.

The Compromise of 1850, whose passage Douglas managed, implicitly applied Popular Sovereignty to the former Mexican provinces of Upper California and New Mexico—the southwestern corner of the present United States. By the Compromise, California entered the Union directly and as a free state. By making no mention of slavery regarding territorial government in New Mexico, Congress effectively allowed its residents to determine slavery's status there. Although the Compromise failed to satisfy fire-eaters, Douglas had the support of seven of the states of the future Confederacy when he unsuccessfully sought the Democratic presidential nomination at Cincinnati in 1856, and the convention made his doctrine a central feature of its platform.

In the previous two years, Douglas had appeased the South in another way: submission of a bill creating two new territories, Kansas and Nebraska, from the still-unorganized parts of the Louisiana Purchase and leaving to their residents the decision on the status of slavery in each one. Under Southern pressure, Douglas's bill also explicitly repealed the Missouri Compromise, despite his recognition that it had become "canonised [sic] in the hearts of the American people, as a sacred thing, which no ruthless hand would ever be reckless enough to disturb."[5]

As Douglas anticipated, the Kansas-Nebraska Act enraged the North, unexpectedly producing the anti-Nebraska movement that fed creation of the Republican Party. As evidence of the way that Southern demands put Northern politicians at risk, his reckless act lost Douglas the support of Midwestern Democrats—and the nomination—at the 1856 Democratic convention. Realizing he could deadlock the convention but not gain its nomination, Douglas put party ahead of personal ambition and threw his support to James Buchanan, his principal competitor and the next president.

Despite those efforts to oblige the South, events in Kansas soon caused fire-eaters to charge Douglas with betrayal. With the status of slavery in the new territory put up for grabs by the application of Popular Sovereignty, Missourians crossed the border to vote illegally and give a proslavery minority control of the Kansas territorial legislature, which promptly passed a slave code. Fraud similarly marred election of the territory's proslavery constitutional convention. That body, which assembled in Lecompton, recognized that the territory's antislavery majority would reject a proslavery constitution in a fair election and therefore sought approval of its work in a referendum giving voters the opportunity to do no more than prohibit the *further* importation of slaves. Those already in the state as well as their progeny would remain bound for life.

Though proslavery forces thus made a sham of democracy—and Popular Sovereignty—the South and the Buchanan administration, eager to admit a new slave state, attempted to force the Lecompton constitution on unwilling Kansans. That assault on representative government Douglas could not abide, and he led the successful congressional resistance to a Kansas statehood bill that included the hated proslavery constitution. "The only question," according to Douglas, "is whether the constitution formed at Lecompton is the act & will of the people of Kansas, [or] whether it be the act and will of a small minority, who have attempted to cheat & defraud the majority by trickery & juggling." It clearly being the latter, the attempt and the bill "must be rebuked." Having nailed his "colors to the mast" of popular government, Douglas won renewed praise in the North even as he earned the hatred of Southern radicals.[6] They and Buchanan's Northern supporters consequently joined to crush Douglas if they could, removing his allies from patronage appointments, stripping him of his committee chairmanship, and attempting to exclude him from the Democratic caucus.

Douglas's response to the *Dred Scott* decision confirmed Southern radicals in their new-found distrust, even though he agreed with Chief Justice Roger Taney that the nation's Founders had not placed blacks on a level of equality with whites. To reassure Midwestern opponents of slavery's expansion, the too-clever Douglas attempted to sidestep Taney's claim that no mere territorial legislature could bar slavery. Responding to Taney's decision and, later, to a question posed by Lincoln during their 1858 debate at Freeport, Illinois, Douglas asserted that no judicial decision could force a community to adopt a slave code. Should it refuse to do so, no slaveholder, Douglas reasoned, would put his human property at risk by taking slaves to an area without laws protecting his ownership. That "Freeport Doctrine" suggested that Taney's decision had awarded the South "a barren and a worthless right"—the right to own slaves in a territory where that right was not "sustained, protected, and enforced by appropriate police regulations and local legislation."[7] Popular Sovereignty lived. Fire-eaters yelled fraud.

Despite his defection over the Lecompton constitution and his warning to Southerners that "it is folly for you to entertain visionary dreams that you can fix slavery where the people do not want it," Douglas did not immediately lose all his support in the South.[8] Rather than see Lincoln elected, the South favored Douglas's return to the Senate in 1858, and conservatives such as future Confederate vice president Alexander Stephens considered the fire-eaters' 1860 attacks on Douglas a "trumped-up war."[9]

To Southern radicals, however, Douglas's Freeport Doctrine effectively nullified the Kansas-Nebraska Act, the *Dred Scott* decision, and the Democrats' Cincinnati platform. Unlike Douglas, who favored expansion as a means to extend popular government, their intention was to spread slavery and Southern institutions despite the preferences of a territory's residents. There was no compromising. Douglas must go, and Alabama fire-eater William Yancey determined to send him on his way, along with his party, if the Democratic platform failed to demand a federal slave code establishing and protecting slavery in the territories. With such a code, a territory could choose to bar slavery only when it applied for statehood, but with it already established that might be less likely.

〰 In one of life's ironies, Yancey, like Douglas, spent his youth in the burned-over evangelical and abolitionist district running from Vermont due west across upstate New York.[10] Shortly after Yancey's birth—the year after Douglas's—young William's father moved his family from Georgia to South Carolina, where he had once shared an Abbeville law office with John Calhoun. After his father's death from yellow fever in the boy's third year, his mother returned to Georgia and later enrolled her children in the academy run by the Reverend Nathan Beman, a transplanted New Englander. Then, in William's seventh year, Mrs. Yancey married the schoolmaster, who soon sold her slaves and moved his new family to a pastorate in Troy, New York. The future Prince of Fire-Eaters, given a good education by his step-father, would be raised in the home of a revivalist preacher and active abolitionist.

Environment had no more influence on Yancey than it did on Douglas. After withdrawing (or being expelled) from Williams College in 1833, Yancey settled in Greenville, South Carolina, where he studied law under Benjamin Perry, the state's leading unionist. There he developed his oratorical style while criticizing John Calhoun for pursuing "*disunion* and a *Southern Confederacy*."[11] After the nullification controversy quieted, Yancey married into Greenville's wealthy Earle family, acquiring both a wife and thirty-five slaves. Newly affluent, he abandoned the law and headed for Alabama to begin life as a planter in the vicinity of an uncle, Jesse Beene, an outspoken advocate of state's rights.

Disaster soon changed the course of Yancey's life. The Panic of 1837 depressed cotton prices, and two years later a neighbor's overseer poisoned his slaves. With most of them dead and the rest too weak to work, Yancey abandoned planting. After serving a short jail sentence for manslaughter as a result of brawling with one of his wife's relatives, he resumed the study of law in 1840 and, with his younger brother, managed a newspaper that championed Jacksonian Democracy, state's rights, and John Calhoun. The paper's support of the presidential candidacy of Martin Van Buren endeared Yancey to local Democrats, who sent him to the state legislature in 1841. For defending the interests of small farmers, he won an 1844 special election to fill a vacant congressional seat. In Washington, Yancey fell further under Calhoun's spell and joined Douglas in opposing protective tariffs but advocating acquisition of Texas and Oregon.

Yancey's advocacy of territorial expansion lacked, however, Douglas's nationalistic and popular fervor. The Alabaman supported expansion in order to add new slave states and block what he regarded as abolitionist New England's efforts to limit Southern influence in the national government. Unlike Douglas, who regarded the Union as a sacred vessel essential to national progress, Yancey considered it no more than "a cluster of Governments" that had yielded certain powers but otherwise retained full sovereignty.[12] Reelected to a full term in 1844, Yancey developed a typical Southern radical's aversion to political parties and resigned his seat in mid-1846 to dedicate himself to state's rights and helping Alabama chart its own course.

Back home, Yancey moved his family to Montgomery, where he practiced law with a relative of Barnwell Rhett and remained active in state politics. Even so, he returned to the national spotlight in 1848 when he co-authored the Alabama Platform. Reversing the traditional Southern claim that Congress lacked authority to legislate regarding slavery in the territories, the platform demanded that Congress use its powers to ensure that "all citizens of the United States together with their property of every description [that is, slaves] . . . remain protected" there.[13] Repudiating any interference with slavery by congressional free soilers, the platform called upon Congress to give full protection to territorial slave ownership. Although Alabama Democrats had instructed their delegates to the 1848 Democratic national convention to reject any candidate not pledged to provide that protection, only Yancey—and one other delegate—walked out when the convention ignored the threat. A dozen years before the party's 1860 convention, Yancey had tested the tactic that wounded Douglas and shattered the Democratic Party when it later met in Charleston.

Yancey did not attend the 1850 Nashville Convention of nine slave states, but he did have high praise for Rhett's closing address. Then, in August, he made a trip to Macon, Georgia, where the two men first met when they were invited to address a gathering called to oppose passage of the Compromise of 1850. When Congress, guided by Douglas, approved the Compromise the next month, Yancey began in earnest his work for secession. That fall, he organized city and county Southern Rights associations, and during their February 1851 convocation in Montgomery he warned that failure to diffuse slaves into the new territories meant black overpopulation in the present slave states and the flight of their white labor. Confining slavery would also reduce the South to a permanent minority within the Union and inevitably end in abolition and race war. The South, Yancey asserted, had no "middle ground between *submission* and *secession*." The delegates agreed. Favoring secession, and reducing the remaining issues to matters "of time and policy only," they called upon the slave states to secede and send representatives to Montgomery.[14]

Once again, Yancey had gotten ahead of himself—by a full decade. Unionists soon gained the upper hand in Alabama, as in John Quitman's Mississippi, and South Carolina refused to secede alone. Southerners, Yancey concluded, would presently go no further than the Georgia Platform expressing conditional acceptance of the Compromise of 1850. That platform committed Georgia to leave the Union if Congress took any one of several actions: 1) abolition of slavery in the District of Columbia or any federal property within a slave state; 2) suppression of the domestic slave trade; 3) rejection of any new slave states; 4) prohibition of slavery's introduction in the territories of New Mexico or Utah; or 5) weakening of the fugitive slave law. Frustrated that secession remained out of reach, Yancey turned his attention to the practice of law and awaited a more favorable moment, some event that might prompt secession.

While he waited, Yancey attended the 1858 Southern commercial convention in Montgomery, where he again saw Rhett as well as Virginia fire-eater Edmund Ruffin, to whose scheme to establish the League of United Southerners the Alabaman gave enthusiastic support. The League might become, Yancey hoped, the vehicle for secession. As he wrote James S. Slaughter, "If we could do as our fathers did, organize committees of public safety all over the cotton States . . . we shall fire the Southern heart—instruct the Southern mind—give courage to each other, and at the proper moment, by one organized, concerted action, we can precipitate the cotton States into a Revolution."[15] Meeting in annual conventions, the League would substitute, Yancey hoped, for political parties, obtaining from Congress guarantees of Southern rights or clearing the way for Southern independence. Though the Ruffin-Yancey effort gave support to Northern belief in a secessionist conspiracy, the League scheme soon collapsed. For his next act of agitation, at the 1860 Charleston Democratic convention, Yancey prepared with greater care.

∽ The Democratic Party had not chosen wisely when selecting Charleston as the site for its nominating convention.[16] Though stressed by controversies over Kansas, the *Dred Scott* decision, the Freeport Doctrine, and reactions to the Harpers Ferry raid, the party had reason to expect victory that fall if only it could remain united. Needing 152 electoral votes to win the presidency, the Democrats anticipated 120 from the slave states and 7 more in California and Oregon. Victory in either New York or Pennsylvania would put its candidate over the top. Success in Douglas's home state of Illinois, nearby Indiana, and any one of the less populous free states would produce the same result. Charleston, however, put at risk the weakened party's search for harmony. Due to poor access, many delegates arrived exhausted, only to face hundred-degree heat, severe crowding, and hotel and meal rates so high that many Northerners lacked financial resources for an extended convention while Southerners enjoyed the hospitality of city friends. More irritating yet, Charlestonians openly displayed their hatred of Northerners, especially Douglas men, and shouted for the South to stand firm against any compromise on a federal slave code.

The political strategies of the party's factions also spelled trouble. Those, North and South, who had supported the Buchanan administration's fight with Douglas over Kansas statehood aimed to block the Little Giant's nomination. Scheming to make selection of a candidate the first order of business, the administration's faction intended to deadlock the convention, cast aside Douglas, and nominate a dark horse. Yancey's allies, the South's radicals, also sought to crush Douglas, but they joined with delegates pledged to the Illinois senator to demand that the convention first agree on a platform.

The Yancey and Douglas factions had different reasons for preferring early action on the platform. The Little Giant's backers wanted to recommit the party to Popular Sovereignty and recapture its Jacksonian character by purging its radical members and remaking it as a truly national rather than largely Southern sectional party. They might accomplish that if Southern radicals bolted the convention over the platform. Yanceyites would then bear the onus of insurgency, and their departure would help Douglas gain the two-thirds' majority needed for nomination.

Though Yancey had accepted Popular Sovereignty in 1856, the subsequent Freeport Doctrine made it a sham in Southern eyes. He therefore demanded that Democrats call upon Congress—and Northerners—to yield to the South by imposing a federal slave code on any territory whose legislature failed to protect slavery. Aware that Douglas had stated he would refuse to run on such a platform, Yanceyites hoped that an early platform victory would drive Douglas supporters from the party and make way for a Southern nominee.

Yancey had made the platform central to his strategy sometime before his visit to Charleston in 1859. While there, he coordinated plans with Rhett and South Carolina radicals and urged them to drop the tariff issue because Southerners would never accept it as grounds for secession. Slavery was the issue, he claimed, and Southerners must defend it at all costs "or all go down together." Though he had no wish to preserve the Union, Yancey urged radicals to work with Southerners who did because cooperation provided an opportunity "to indoctrinate all parties in our midst with [radical] constitutional views." Cooperation would also enable the minority of fire-eaters to dominate the convention, crush Douglas, and bend Northerners to their will.[17] If not, a united South could destroy the Democratic Party, ensure Lincoln's election, and use that as pretext for disunion. Rhett and Yancey had found their issue; it might create that event for which they had longed.

Back in Alabama, Yancey maneuvered to control his state's convention, recommit it to the 1848 Alabama Platform, and pledge its delegation to leave the convention if Democrats rejected a territorial slave code. Perhaps influenced by John Brown's raid, trial, and execution, the Alabama convention accepted Yancey's stratagems. To strengthen his hand, Yancey met with the delegations from Arkansas and all Deep South states save South Carolina on the eve of the Charleston convention. Uniformly opposed to Douglas, each delegation agreed to join Alabama's withdrawal should the convention reject a slave-code platform.

Douglas supporters arrived in Charleston no less determined to succeed than Yanceyites. In the interests of harmony, their man had graciously stepped aside in 1852 and 1856 and thereafter campaigned hard to elect the party's nominee. Now it was his turn, and they meant him to have it. They also meant to have a platform capable of stopping the Northern Democrats' slide into political oblivion. Expecting only a few Southern delegations to bolt, they tried to appease Southern moderates with a guarantee of slavery where it existed and a commitment to acquire Cuba. To satisfy Northern voters, Douglasites insisted on the party's 1856 Cincinnati platform favoring Popular Sovereignty.

Despite an impassioned speech by Yancey, the convention narrowly approved the Douglas platform. Having won, the Little Giant's supporters offered yet another olive branch designed to secure their man's nomination. In a virtual surrender of their platform victory, they received overwhelming approval—the Deep South abstaining—for a plank pledging Democratic support for any future Supreme Court decision limiting a territorial legislature's authority to bar slavery.

With five Southern Democrats dominating the Court, Yancey might have declared victory and helped his party proceed to nomination of a candidate. After some indecision and an angry exchange with the next speaker, Leroy Walker instead led the Alabama delegates from the hall. They were followed by those of Mississippi, Louisiana, South Carolina (which had not intended to leave until taunted beyond endurance by Charlestonians in the galleries), Florida, Texas, a few from Delaware and Arkansas, and, the next day, Georgia's and the rest of those from Arkansas. Had Caleb Cushing, chairman of the rump convention, not ruled that nomination required two-thirds of the original number of delegates, the convention might have quickly nominated Douglas. Instead, the tally for the Little Giant fell short, again and again. After fifty-seven ballots, his supporters voted to reconvene in Baltimore on June 18.

Those who walked out reassembled nearby where, lacking leadership, they reflected on their situation. Radicals wanted to split the party, which should help elect Lincoln and facilitate secession. Others, equally calculating, hoped that two Democratic candidates would deadlock the Electoral College, thus giving the South a victory in the House and Senate that it could not win at the ballot box. Others anticipated that their departure would undermine support for Douglas and cause the convention to invite their return for nomination of a compromise candidate.

According to historian David Potter, most of those who bolted the convention were hardly so rational. The majority, he claimed, simply reacted to secessionist rhetoric, ultraradical Charleston crowds, and "gusts of emotion." In an overexcited state, they thoughtlessly "took positions which led on to consequences that they did not visualize."[18] When not promptly invited to rejoin the convention, the bolters engaged in much mutual recrimination before deciding to consult with their state party organizations and to reconvene in Richmond on June 11. Despite some minor adjustments, those consultations denied Douglas men control of any of the returning delegations, though in Alabama, Arkansas, Georgia, and Louisiana irregular party meetings added them to existing delegations or appointed new ones favoring the Little Giant.

Except for a newly elected and more radical South Carolina delegation, which refused to go to Baltimore, the former bolters merely passed through Richmond en route to Maryland for the reconvened regular Democratic convention. Once there, they walked out again when that body voted to give to the pro-Douglas factions all of Alabama's and Louisiana's seats, half of Georgia's, and some of Arkansas's. This time, Virginia, North Carolina, Tennessee, half of Maryland, California, Oregon, and most of Kentucky, Missouri, and Arkansas joined the Deep South's exodus.

Seeking to prevent such a party-shattering outcome, Douglas had twice written his agents to withdraw his name. Resentful of years of Southern demands, whose acceptance had nearly destroyed the Midwestern wing of their party, the Little Giant's managers refused. When their man still fell short of the two-thirds requirement, if measured against the original number of delegates, the regular convention simply ignored that rule and approved a June 23 resolution declaring Douglas unanimously nominated.

The same day, the bolters, plus a few delegates from the Northeast, convened in Baltimore's Market Hall to nominate John Breckinridge and approve a platform modeled on resolutions that

Jefferson Davis had proposed to the Senate in February 1860.[19] That platform, though not demanding immediate enactment of a federal slave code, obligated Congress to impose one on a territory if necessary to protect slave property. For an election that thoughtful observers believed would determine the fate of the Union, Douglas and Breckinridge, supported by the pieces of the now-broken Democratic Party, joined two other candidates already in the field.

NOTES

1. Charleston *Mercury*, May 3, 1860.

2. This and the following paragraphs describing the career of Stephen Douglas rest upon Robert W. Johannsen, *Stephen A. Douglas* (New York: Oxford University Press, 1973).

3. Douglas, orally, to Murray McConnell in April 1854 quoted in Johannsen, *Douglas*, 419.

4. Douglas quoted in ibid., 275.

5. Douglas quoted in ibid., 255.

6. Douglas quoted in ibid., 581 and 588.

7. Douglas quoted in ibid., 569.

8. Don E. Fehrenbacher, *Slavery, Law, and Politics: The Dred Scott Case in Historical Perspective* (Oxford: Oxford University Press, 1981), 244–63, regarded Douglas's Freeport Doctrine as less damning in Southern eyes than his defeat of the South's efforts to make Kansas a slave state, his opposition to a federal slave code, and his 1858 refusal to answer Lincoln's repeated questions about an appropriate response to a hypothetical Supreme Court decision forcing free states to accept slave ownership. Douglas quoted in ibid., 246.

9. Thomas E. Schott, *Alexander H. Stephens of Georgia: A Biography* (Baton Rouge: Louisiana State University Press, 1988), 294.

10. This section on Yancey's life is based upon Eric Walther, *The Fire-Eaters* (Baton Rouge: Louisiana State University Press, 1992), 48–82. See also Clement Eaton, *The Mind of the Old South* (Baton Rouge: Louisiana State University Press, 1964), 202–21, and John Witherspoon DuBose, *The Life and Times of William Lowndes Yancey* (1892; reprint ed., New York: Peter Smith, 1942).

11. Yancey quoted in Walther, *Fire-Eaters*, 51.

12. Yancey quoted in ibid., 55.

13. Alabama Platform quoted in Eaton, *Mind of the South*, 207.

14. Yancey and the association resolution quoted in Walther, *Fire-Eaters*, 61.

15. Yancey quoted in ibid., 71.

16. For this section on the 1860 Democratic convention see Walther, *Fire-Eaters*, 72–76; David S. Heidler, *Pulling the Temple Down: The Fire-Eaters and the Destruction of the Union* (Mechanicsburg, PA: Stackpole

Books, 1994), 139–59; David M. Potter, *The Impending Crisis, 1848–1861* (New York: Harper & Row, 1976), 405–15; Roy F. Nichols, *The Disruption of American Democracy* (New York: Macmillan, 1948), 270–322; and Allan Nevins, *The Emergence of Lincoln*, vol. 2, *Prologue to Civil War, 1859–1861* (New York: Scribner's, 1950), 203–28.

17. Yancey quoted in Walther, *Fire-Eaters*, 72. On Rhett's reaction to Yancey's strategy see Heidler, *Pulling the Temple Down*, 139–41, and Laura A. White, *Robert Barnwell Rhett: Father of Secession* (New York: Century, 1931; reprint, 1965), 154–55.

18. Potter, *Impending Crisis*, 414.

19. On the role of Jefferson Davis see William C. Davis, *Jefferson Davis: The Man and His Hour* (New York: HarperCollins, 1991), 282. James A. Rawley, *Secession: The Disruption of the American Republic, 1844–1861* (Malabar, FL: Krieger, 1960), 224–25, reprints relevant portions of the platform.

CHAPTER FIVE

THE MEN OF THE WEST AND THE ELECTION OF 1860

The Constitution and the equality of the states!
These are the symbols of everlasting union.
Let these be the rallying cries of the people.
—John Breckinridge[1]

IN THE MONTH after the Democrats disintegrated at Charleston, two other parties convened to write platforms and name presidential candidates. The first to do so, the Constitutional Union Party, was a new growth on conservative roots. Cultivated by a Kentucky Whig, Senator John Crittenden, and nourished by growing evidence of Democratic schism, plans for a new conservative coalition quickly took shape in 1859. By February of the next year, Crittenden and his associates had broadcast an appeal to voters calling for the formation of a new party because neither of the others could be "safely entrusted with the management of public affairs."[2] Other than political opportunity, one thing united Crittenden and his colleagues: They aimed to save the Union.

Between his group's first meeting in December 1858 and the new party's May 1860 convention in Baltimore, Crittenden drew into his alliance remnants of the Northern states' Whig organizations and many former Southern Whigs, at that time often running for office as the Opposition Party. He also coordinated his plans with representatives of the American (Know-Nothing) Party, an anti-Catholic, anti-immigrant organization that arose in the early 1850s, contended with Republicans for the votes of former Northern Whigs, and ran well in the Border and Upper South in 1856.

By taking no position on slavery, the Constitutional Union Party created an illusion of consensus, which it hoped would appeal to unionists everywhere. That stance enabled those speaking on the party's behalf to spell out its commitment to "the Constitution of the Country, the Union of the States, and the Enforcement of the Laws" as would best suit local voters, even if their interpretations might not bear close comparison.[3] Still, with the status of slavery virtually settled in all present territories, a Constitutional Union victory might—the fire-eaters willing—have kept the issue out of Congress for some years and left the illusion unchallenged.

In an attempt to draw conservatives from all sections, the party quickly settled on John Bell, a Tennessee Whig, as its presidential nominee and Edward Everett of Massachusetts as his running mate. A slaveholder employing several hundred bondsmen in his mines and rolling mill, Bell had for years quietly defended slavery against the worst abolitionist attacks, and unionists hoped that slave-state voters would help elect him as they had Louisiana's slaveholding military hero, Zachary Taylor, in 1848.

Northern conservatives might find much to admire in Bell's public career. He had opposed the Mexican War and played an important role in passage of the Compromise of 1850. Bell had also voted against the congressional gag rule that for a decade had denied abolitionists their First Amendment right to petition Congress. In addition, he had opposed both the Kansas-Nebraska Act and President James Buchanan's attempt to force the "[un]fairly formed" Lecompton constitution on antislavery Kansans. Unlike most Southern leaders, Bell also acknowledged that Congress had some power over slavery in the territories and the District of Columbia, where he was willing to see it abolished if that would quiet the "ill-judged agitation [and] officious intervention of Northern fanatics."[4]

Although the son of a blacksmith and farmer living near Nashville, Tennessee, Bell had attended Cumberland College, from which he was graduated in 1814. Though never brilliant, and one who reached conclusions only after much thought, he read for the law, became a member of the Tennessee bar, and began his public career with election to the state senate in 1817. After marrying into the wealthy Dickinson and Murfree families, he moved his law practice to Nashville, where he became well acquainted with the state's leaders. Like most Tennesseans, Bell resented Andrew

Jackson's defeat in the election of 1824, and he soon announced his intention to run for Congress as a Jacksonian Democrat.

As a member of the House, Bell initially gave enthusiastic support to Jackson's policies and, as chairman of the Judiciary Committee, pushed through the Force Bill authorizing the president to crush South Carolina for its 1832 attempt to nullify the federal tariff. After Jackson's veto of the bill rechartering the Bank of the United States put Bell at odds with his president, the congressman approached open opposition when a minority of Democrats joined with Whigs to make him Speaker of the House. Bell completed his break with the Jacksonians when he favored Hugh Lawson White, a Tennessee friend, over Martin Van Buren as the Democratic presidential nominee in 1836. Hoping (in a preview of a Bell strategy in 1860) to throw the election of a president into the House, the Whig Party unsuccessfully ran several regional favorite sons. When one of those candidates, William Henry Harrison, won four years later, Bell became his secretary of war, but Harrison's sudden death sent Bell back to Tennessee until his election to the Senate in 1847.

Perceiving a grave threat to the Union as early as 1851, Bell became interested in the formation of a unionist coalition of conservatives from all sections. With the Whig Party collapsing and the new American Party objectionably nativist, he saw little prospect of success and took no direct part in Crittenden's efforts to create the Constitutional Union Party. Bell nevertheless quickly fell in with efforts to name him its presidential candidate.

〰️ Eight days after Bell's nomination, the Republican Party convened in Chicago. Despite the hoopla from throngs of supporters come to shout for their favorites, the delegates solemnly approved a platform praising the Union as the source of national prosperity and guarantor of republican institutions. Attempting to reassure the South, the platform writers affirmed each state's right to determine its domestic institutions (meaning slavery) and, with John Brown in mind, denounced as "the gravest of crimes" the "lawless invasion by armed force . . . of any state or territory."[5]

After condemning the Buchanan administration for attempting to force slavery on Kansas, the platform addressed issues setting Republicans apart from their opponents. Asserting that the nation's Founders had intended the territories for freedom, the platform denied the authority of "Congress, of a territorial legislature, or of any individuals" (justices of the Supreme Court?) "to give legal existence to slavery in any territory of the United States." With the November election's key constituencies in mind, it closed with support for free homesteads, protective tariffs, agricultural colleges, fair treatment of the foreign born, and federal money for rivers, harbors, and a Pacific railroad.

Selection of a candidate moved forward in a spirit not found in Charleston the previous month. That might not have been the case, for the North too had its political divisions. The upper North, stretching from New England through upstate New York to Minnesota, supported the strongly antislavery candidacy of New York's William Seward. Bordering on slave territory, the lower North states running westward from New Jersey and Pennsylvania to Iowa favored various party moderates. Recognizing that any likely nominee would carry the upper North, several of New England's leaders, putting victory above all else, demanded that the convention approve a candidate who could win in the states along the Southern border. Why? Adding the electoral votes of Pennsylvania and either Illinois, Indiana, or New Jersey to John Frémont's 1856 total would bring victory.

In the balloting, Seward began strongly, but Abraham Lincoln's managers energetically united the scattered opposition to close the gap. With party leaders concluding that Lincoln—and the tariff—could carry Illinois and Pennsylvania into the Republican column on November 6, he made dramatic gains on the second ballot. When the third round left Lincoln only one and one-half votes short of a majority, Ohio switched four of its votes to give him the nomination. Whatever might later be said of their candidate during the campaign, Republicans had chosen a moderate, one sympathetic to the South, born in Kentucky, raised among Southern emigrants in Indiana, and, like Douglas, married into a slaveowning family.

～⁀ John Breckinridge, the last of the four contestants to be named, had the easiest route to nomination. Though with a bit of effort he might have become the compromise candidate of a united Democratic Party, Breckinridge had held his supporters in check and looked forward to taking his new seat in the Senate. Only when Democratic division had become unavoidable did he release them—in time to give him the unwanted nomination of the Southern Democrats.* To a handful of Northeastern Democrats Breckinridge had recently disavowed secession, and they joined those who had bolted at Baltimore to put his name in nomination. He won easily, right after the bolters approved the slave-code platform rejected at Charleston. Though for two terms an able and well-liked member of the House of Representatives, a superb speaker, and a popular vice president to Buchanan, Breckinridge seems a strange choice for the party of secession, even if the Kentuckian owned a handful slaves. His candidacy, as his close friend John Forney observed, was "a curious sequel in a life which opened in 1851 in Congress in avowed sympathy with the anti-slavery idea."[6]

From grandparents on both sides, Breckinridge had inherited views on slavery anathema to fire-eaters. His grandfather Breckinridge, a state's rights ally of Jefferson's, joined the Virginian in confessing slavery an evil that harmed both blacks and whites and must eventually be abolished. His maternal grandfather Witherspoon held similar beliefs, and Breckinridge's parents honored the family's antislavery tradition. While attending Princeton, his father had assimilated antislavery views from college president Samuel Smith, his eventual father-in-law, and roomed with future Kentucky abolitionist James Birney, whom Salmon Chase would defend in Ohio's courts.

Unsurprisingly then, young Breckinridge formed his first friendships among soft-on-slavery Southern conservatives. In Lexington his early playmates included both Mary Todd, who would marry his 1860 Republican rival, and the children of future Whig senator John Crittenden, inspiration of the Constitutional Union Party. At Centre College, Breckinridge grew close to David Birney, son of the abolitionist, whose home Breckinridge

---

*The Democratic National Executive Committee, a variation of the traditional National Democratic Executive Committee used by Douglas, managed the Breckinridge campaign. To avoid confusing and cumbersome terminology, the two Democratic parties will hereinafter be referred to as Northern and Southern Democrats.

often visited. While in Princeton reading for the law, Breckinridge lived with his Uncle Robert, a life-long influence and member of the American Colonization Society. Strange companions for the future candidate of the party of secession!

As a one-term Kentucky legislator, two-term congressman, and Buchanan's vice president, Breckinridge seems to have held quietly to the Jeffersonian view of slavery as a necessary evil and rejected the proslavery views popular in the South after 1830. He also remained close to his antislavery uncles and had among his close friends several emancipationists. As a Mason and member of Lexington's First Presbyterian Church, he attached himself to other institutions opposing slavery, and he continued to favor freedom for slaves—if it led to their colonization. During Mary Todd Lincoln's frequent visits with her Lexington relatives, he even drew Abraham Lincoln into his circle of close acquaintances.

Though Breckinridge never concealed from Kentucky voters his doubts about slavery, in public life he conformed to Southern views. He spoke against abolition of slavery in the District of Columbia and its exclusion from territories south of an extended Missouri Compromise line. As a congressional conservative, Breckinridge supported the Compromise of 1850—including the end of slave trading in the District of Columbia, California's entry as a free state, and organization of the rest of the Mexican Cession on the basis of Popular Sovereignty. Having taken that step toward sectional peace, he then played a major role, along with Secretary of War Jefferson Davis, in blasting national harmony when helping to convince Douglas and President Franklin Pierce to include explicit repeal of the Missouri Compromise in the Kansas-Nebraska Act.

Repeated abolitionist attacks and his nomination for the vice presidency in 1856 caused Breckinridge to harden his views, though he continued to regard slavery as immoral. He began to offer a legalistic and historical defense of slavery and the slave-owners' right to benefit from the territories, which he described as the common property of all the states. During the presidential campaign, he interpreted the Cincinnati platform to mean that territories might not bar slavery until applying for statehood. Still, he denied any intention to force the institution upon them, though warning Northern voters that continued attempts to exclude it would extinguish "the last spark of affection between the North and the South" and make the Union "hateful and intolerable."[7]

As vice president, Breckinridge described the Republican Party as a "most dangerous, atrocious, and baneful organization," and he ignored the illegal voting by Missourians that gave Kansas a proslavery territorial legislature.[8] He also overlooked the gerrymandering and electoral fraud in the election of Kansas's proslavery constitutional convention, and, unlike Bell, he offered no objection to President Buchanan's efforts to impose the Lecompton constitution on antislavery Kansans. On that record, the Kentucky legislature selected Breckinridge to fill a Senate vacancy opening in 1861. Before taking office, however, he had a rendezvous with those who had bolted from the Democratic conventions in Charleston and Baltimore.

~ If the Southern Democrats' rejection of Stephen Douglas and their nomination of John Breckinridge appeared to represent the South's triumph over the Midwest, the final slate of presidential candidates and the shift of America's population center portended otherwise. In 1860 the nation's center of population moved from Virginia, one of the original and slaveowning states, to Ohio, carved out of the territory from which Congress had barred slavery in 1787.[9] Political power seemed about to migrate in the same direction.

The home states of the four presidential candidates suggested that fundamental trends had turned against the South and its continued domination of the federal government. Only four of the nation's first fifteen presidents had resided west of the Appalachians at the time of their election. Even those four had been born in the East—Virginia or the Carolinas—and three were prominent as much for military heroism as for being men of the West. Reflecting the South's political dominance in the nation's first seven decades, eight of those first fifteen presidents were Southerners who, collectively, held the office during forty-nine of the seventy-two years since George Washington's inauguration.

Viewed from the perspective of the upcoming presidential campaign, the South's rejection of Douglas suggests not superior strength but the last gasp of an old order. In 1860 all four presidential candidates resided in western states of the upper South or lower North, and all save Douglas had been born there. Within the White House, at least, the election would shift the geographical center of power westward—and possibly northward—along with the center of population.

The demise of the national political parties, as evidenced by the emergence of four major candidates, also foretold a shift in the sectional shares of federal power. Because of the nation's single-member congressional districts and the widespread practice of giving a state's entire electoral vote to the candidate with a plurality of its popular vote, American elections tended to become two-man affairs. Voting for minor candidates whose parties had little chance of electing a president, congressman, or governor struck most citizens as a waste of their vote. The structure of the federal government, with its divided and shared legislative and executive powers, reinforced that two-party tendency and helped make those parties national in scope. Unless a party fielded candidates on a platform giving them some chance of success in all parts of the Union, it had little hope of winning enough state and district elections to gain control of both houses of Congress and put its man in the White House. Without all those prizes, the party could hardly expect to turn its electoral platform into legislation and see it implemented by a sympathetic executive.

The resulting national two-party system had an important advantage: it encouraged the parties to offer platforms representing broad compromises not only between economic and social groups within a district or state but also among the rapidly expanding nation's various sections. A party platform highly pleasing to voters in one part of the country, such as a vigorous defense or condemnation of slavery, would likely subject its candidates elsewhere to certain defeat. Only through compromises acceptable to all sections might a party hope to gain control of the federal government. Forming those compromises meant that parties usually disciplined their most extreme members, who by taking stands popular only at home might put national harmony—and party success—to the test.

The collapse of both Whigs and Democrats and the emergence of the sectional Republican and Southern Democratic parties consequently had dire implications for the Union. No less momentous, at least for the South, was the Democratic disruption. Even as the Whigs weakened, Southern representatives had remained a majority within the Democratic congressional caucuses. So long as the party had a significant Northern wing, Democrats could maintain their majority position within the Congress and permit Southern-dominated caucuses to appoint committee chairmen and control the flow of congressional legislation. As Southern Democrats cast aside Northerners, however, they facilitated a shift of federal power against them—a movement of no concern to radicals seeking Southern salvation in independence.

In 1860 no party matched the Republicans' organization or finances. Douglas had only scattered strength in the South, and Breckinridge similarly lacked support in the North. The two Democrats also divided funding from traditional party sources. From bits and pieces of the American and old Whig parties, Bell struggled to create an organization. Though wealthy businessmen liked him and his platform, they found little reason to fund a probable loser. In June, however, none of the candidates believed that he faced certain defeat. Republicans expected to hold the eleven states that Frémont had won in 1856 and elect Lincoln with victories in Pennsylvania and Illinois. In defiance of that strategy, Douglas thought to carry most of the North by convincing voters that they must chose either him and the Union or Lincoln and secession, which fire-eaters threatened would follow the Republican's election. A few victories in the upper South could then make Douglas president. Bell and Breckinridge supporters, the latter including traditional Democratic voters as well as fire-eaters, believed that they could win overwhelmingly in the slave states and move into the White House with victories in the lower North.

As the campaign developed, however, Douglas quickly perceived that he would run second to Lincoln in the North, and Bell and Breckinridge realized that they would divide the South between them. Prompted by those assessments, Lincoln's opponents began considering other strategies. Some Bell and Breckinridge backers hoped to deny Lincoln a majority in the Electoral College and elect a Southern president in the House. That could occur because, should the election be decided there, the Constitution called for each state's congressmen to cast a single vote. With seventeen needed to elect, Republicans had a majority of the members and the right to cast that vote in only fifteen. Southern Democrats controlled thirteen delegations, Northern Democrats one, and Americans one; no party held the edge in Kentucky, Maryland, or North Carolina. Assuming that Lincoln's total would not grow, Breckinridge could, in theory, add the necessary four votes to his thirteen if he gained the support of one American Party congressman in each of the three equally divided states and the three in Tennessee came out for him. The more likely result, however, was a stalemate in the House. If so, Joseph Lane, Breckinridge's running mate, seemed likely to become acting president when the Democratic majority in the Senate elected him vice president over the Republican candidate. Faced with the latter prospect, perhaps Republicans in the House would elect Bell rather than see Lane become president?

In light of those possibilities, achieving an outcome other than Lincoln's election required defeating the Republican in either New York or New Jersey and Pennsylvania, where President Buchanan used his influence on behalf of Breckinridge. As Bell's and Breckinridge's national managers assessed the chances of doing so, they concluded that their parties must join forces with each other and Douglas to elect in each critical state a common slate of presidential electors. By informal understanding, those electors, if selected by the state's voters, would cast their Electoral College ballots for whichever of the three men—Douglas, Bell, or Breckinridge— had the best chance of stopping Lincoln. Fearing that a three-way division of the anti-Republican presidential vote might defeat Democratic candidates for statewide office, local party leaders sometimes supported the national campaign organizations' hopes for Bell-Douglas-Breckinridge combinations in the lower North.

Even so, fusion faced great obstacles. Though party leaders in New York, Pennsylvania, Rhode Island, and New Jersey agreed on joint slates of electors, dissident Douglasites in Pennsylvania put forth a slate of their own. As that effort suggested, many members of the public showed little interest in fusion's complicated political scheming. They wanted to vote for electors who would support their man, not some unknown one of three. Also complicating hopes for cooperation, Southern Douglas and Bell backers proposed joining forces there to defeat Breckinridge, their putative ally elsewhere.

By midsummer, Douglas perceived that he would run second not only to Lincoln in the upper North but also to Breckinridge in the cotton South and Bell in the upper South. Believing the Union's future to be at risk, Douglas threw presidential tradition aside and waged an exhausting personal campaign. Beginning in upstate New York and New England, Douglas next moved to the southeast—North Carolina, Maryland, and Virginia—and at Norfolk made unmistakably clear his position on secession. Challenged with questions from Breckinridge's local manager, Douglas "emphatically" denied that Lincoln's election justified secession, and he boldly affirmed his belief that "the President . . . , whoever he may be, should treat all attempts to break up the Union . . . as Old Hickory treated the Nullifiers in 1832."[10] Though Douglas asked that the same questions be put to Breckinridge, the Southern Democrat knew that he dare not answer them lest he abandon all hope for success in the North.

Near the end of his subsequent swing through Pennsylvania, New York City, and the Midwest, Douglas concluded from Republican victories in state elections in Vermont and Maine and then in Pennsylvania, Ohio, and Indiana that "Mr. Lincoln is the next President. We must try to save the Union. I will go South."[11] In perhaps his finest hour as an American statesman, Douglas spent the last month of the campaign moving across the Deep South, subjecting himself to insult and exhaustion, dodging over-ripe fruit and rotten eggs, and, when a platform collapsed, suffering physical injury. Still he pushed on, condemning abolition and secession alike and pleading with voters to keep faith with the Union.

Douglas, who acted out of great conviction and in response to a grievous threat to national unity, was not the sole candidate to defend the Union. Lincoln, without reservation, condemned secession, and Bell, with whom Douglas cooperated in the South, ran on a platform devoted to national preservation. Even Breckinridge, the candidate of the South's radicals, proclaimed his support for the Union, if on his own unacceptably Southern terms. He thereby drew, in addition to the votes of fire-eaters, the support of Buchanan men in the North and the South's

Table 1. Popular Vote in Presidential Election of 1860

(in thousands)

(state's and region's winner and percentage in **bold** type)

State/Region	Total Vote	Douglas	Breckinridge		Bell		Lincoln
Alabama	90	14	**49**	**(54%)**	28		–
Florida	13	–	**8**	**(62%)**	5		–
Georgia	107	12	**52**	**(49%)**	43		–
Louisiana	51	8	**23**	**(45%)**	20		–
Mississippi	69	4	**40**	**(58%)**	25		–
South Carolina	No vote; presidential electors, for **Breckinridge**, selected by legislature						
Texas	63	–	**48**	**(76%)**	15		–
Deep South	393	38	**220**	**(56%)**	136		–
Arkansas	54	5	**29**	**(54%)**	20		–
North Carolina	96	3	**49**	**(51%)**	45		–
Tennessee	144	11	64		**69**	**(48%)**	–
Virginia	167	16	74		**74**	**(44%)**	2
Upper South	461	35	**216**	**(47%)**	208		2
Delaware	16	1	**7**	**(44%)**	4		4
Kentucky	146	26	53		**66**	**(45%)**	1
Maryland	93	6	**42**	**(45%)**	42		2
Missouri	165	**59**	**(36%)**	31	58		17
Border South	420	92	133		**170**	**(40%)**	24
Southern total	1,274	165	**569**	**(45%)**	514		26

Source: U.S. Bureau of the Census, *Historical Statistics of the United States: Colonial Times to 1970*, 2 vols. (Washington, DC: U.S. Government Printing Office, 1975), series Y135–186, 2:1077–80.

Jacksonian Democrats, who voted not for secession but for Breckinridge as the candidate of the local party to which they had long been loyal. His failure to disown his secessionist supporters, however, caused many to doubt the sincerity of his statements on behalf of "everlasting union." The San Antonio *Alamo Express*, for example, wrote: "Mr. Breckinridge claims that he isn't a disunionist. An animal not willing to pass for a pig shouldn't stay in the stye."[12]

With the Union at risk, some historians have criticized Republicans for not attempting to avert secession by campaigning in the South, if only to counter the manner in which Breckinridge allowed his radical supporters to demonize Lincoln, whom he knew to be no fiend. We should not thoughtlessly assume, however, that Southerners had no means of learning Lincoln's views, all of which were well summarized in several campaign publications, if they wished or dared to buy and read them. During the campaign, moreover, Lincoln supplemented them as he freely and candidly responded to interviews by Southerners who, Allan Nevins wrote, arrived in Springfield, Illinois, "full of prejudice, but left satisfied with his loyalty to the full constitutional rights of the South."[13] Given the readiness of Southern vigilantes to assault—even lynch—anyone suspected of abolitionism and with slave state laws outlawing criticism of slavery, one might fairly ask how Republicans could have built an organization and campaigned on their platform in the Deep South.[14] The shortcoming seems less the Republicans' than the South's.

As for the Republican failure to inform Northerners about the risk of secession, several points deserve consideration: Douglas was doing that. Because affirming the Little Giant's claim might worry Northerners into rejecting Lincoln, Republicans had little reason to help their opponent. To most Republicans, moreover, secession talk seemed only the latest instance of the Slave Power using threats of disunion to weaken Northern resolve. As Lincoln complacently explained, the "people of the South have too much of good sense, and good temper, to attempt the ruin of the government. . . . At least, so I hope and believe."[15]

The election results (see Table 1) disappointed many voters but surprised few of them. Lincoln held onto his party's 1856 winnings and made big gains in the lower North. Though receiving just over 39 percent of the popular vote, he won all but three of the free states' electoral votes, twenty-seven more than needed. His party's congressional candidates fared less well. Their opponents would outnumber Republicans in both houses of the next Congress, unless some portion of the South seceded and took with it the opposition's edge.

Though fusion tickets make exact counts impossible, Douglas came second in the popular poll but won only a dozen electoral votes—all nine of Missouri's and the three of New Jersey's that had not gone to Lincoln. Breckinridge ran third at the ballot box but won the second spot where it counts with seventy-two electoral votes from the Deep South, Arkansas, North Carolina, Maryland, and Delaware. Bell, with the fewest popular votes, received the thirty-nine electoral votes of Virginia, Tennessee, and Breckinridge's home state of Kentucky. As secessionists swung into action, others worried: What might be the fate of the Union now that Lincoln would become president?

NOTES

1. Breckinridge quoted in William C. Davis, *Breckinridge: Statesman, Soldier, Symbol* (Baton Rouge: Louisiana State University Press, 1974), 231.

2. The appeal quoted in Joseph H. Parks, *John Bell of Tennessee* (Baton Rouge: Louisiana State University Press, 1950), 348–49. The summary of Bell's life and political career in the paragraphs that follow is based upon this biography. On the party conventions and election campaigns as described throughout this chapter see Roy F. Nichols, *The Disruption of American Democracy* (New York: Macmillan, 1948), 288–350; Allan Nevins, *The Emergence of Lincoln*, vol. 2, *Prologue to Civil War, 1859–1861* (New York: Scribner's, 1950), 203–317; David M. Potter, *The Impending Crisis, 1848–1861* (New York: Harper & Row, 1976), 385–447; and Robert W. Johannsen, *Stephen A. Douglas* (New York: Oxford University Press, 1973), 749–807.

3. From the platform as reprinted in James A. Rawley, *Secession: The Disruption of the American Republic, 1844–1861* (Malabar, FL: Krieger, 1990), 226.

4. Bell quoted in Parks, *John Bell*, 327 and 261.

5. The quotations in this and the next paragraph are from the Republican platform as excerpted in Rawley, *Secession*, 227–30.

6. Forney quoted in Davis, *Breckinridge*, 229. The summary of Breckinridge's career and political views found here draws upon pages 3–290 of this biography.

7. Breckinridge quoted in ibid., 156.

8. Breckinridge quoted in ibid., 189.

9. For the movement of the center of population, see the illustration in Nevins, *Emergence of Lincoln*, 310.

10. Douglas quoted in Johannsen, *Douglas*, 788–89.

11. Douglas quoted in ibid., 797–98.

12. Breckinridge and the San Antonio *Alamo Express* quoted in Davis, *Breckinridge*, 231–32.

13. Nevins, *Emergence of Lincoln*, 278.

14. On the silencing of Southern unionists see Nevins, *Emergence of Lincoln*, 287 and 306–9, and Clement Eaton, *The Freedom-of-Thought Struggle in the Old South*, Harper Torchbooks (New York: Harper & Row, 1964), 376–407.

15. Lincoln quoted in Potter, *Impending Crisis*, 432.

CHAPTER SIX

ALEXANDER STEPHENS, DEEP SOUTH SECESSION, AND THE FAILURE OF SOUTHERN UNIONISM

I have no doubt Lincoln is just as good,
safe and sound a man as Mr. Buchanan,
and would administer the Government
so far as he is individually concerned
just as safely for the South. . . . I know the
man well. He is not a bad man.
—Alexander Stephens[1]

ON THE EVE of the cotton states' secession, the Deep South enjoyed a fifteen-year economic boom that had pushed the per capita income of its free population and the average wealth of its farmers ahead of every other region in the nation.[2] Because international demand for cotton had grown sufficiently to sustain prices even as planters boosted output by opening new lands and buying more slaves, the value of the region's principal crop doubled between 1845 and 1860. In addition to higher incomes, slaveholders growing 90 percent of the cotton also saw the value of their human assets multiply when the average price of slaves doubled in those years. Free to prosper and govern, and sustained by the proslavery argument, most planters regarded slavery as the basis of a superior civilization and themselves as its exemplars.

Though political upheaval rarely emerges from the ease and confidence born of power and growing wealth, something beneath the surface troubled residents of the Deep South. In the end, it prompted most to forsake a political system that they had long regarded as the world's best. Something also affected cooler heads, leaving them unable to defeat the rush to secession and force a reasoned assessment of the risks of independence and the merits of the Union.

The fire-eaters' lurid descriptions of the consequences of a Lincoln presidency, and the overwhelming rush of events, help to explain why many Southerners joined the secession crusade in late 1860, eventually enough to make Deep South independence a reality. Horrified by fire-eater polemics, secession's new supporters concluded that the newly elected administration intended to destroy Southern society, degrade and imperil its white citizens, and threaten the planters' right to prosper and rule. The risks, it seemed, lay in remaining within the Union until antislavery blows had begun to fall.

In regard to the national government, secession's supporters feared that the South would soon lose its ability to shape federal policies. With the presidency slipping away, it mattered not to them that a Southern-dominated Democratic Party could still control the government's other branches or that the South—with the aid of policies acceptable to Northern Democratic allies— might again elect a president. Aiming for independence, Deep South radicals instead warned of nothing ahead but antislavery legislation and the appointment of enough justices to end the Supreme Court's proslavery bias. The time for action had come.

Nor did Republicans threaten only Southern control of the federal government. Radicals worried about the loyalty of the South's slaveless yeomanry considered their relative poverty a menace to planter domination of state and local administrations. A mere 5 percent of the region's farm population controlled nearly 40 percent of its agricultural wealth. Focusing only on the even fewer families owning fifty or more slaves, William Barney discovered that they possessed about one-quarter of the cotton South's personal property and somewhat more of its real estate. According to Roger Ransom's sampling, the $33,906 value of the average cotton South slave farm exceeded by fifteen times the worth of its farms operated without benefit of bound labor.

Antebellum visitors to the Deep South regularly observed that the radically uneven distribution of its wealth left many slaveless farm families living in dire poverty with an average wealth barely one-half that of Northern farmers. Should the poor yeomen of the Cotton Kingdom attribute their disadvantage to slavery, might they one day end it? Reject planter rule? Would the newly empowered Republican Party become agent and outlet for their frustrations? Fearing so, Southern governments quickly banned Hinton Helper's 1857 book, *The Impending Crisis of the South*, in which the North Carolinian blamed slavery for the yeomen's distress. Doubting that men could be kept forever in ignorance, a February 1860 correspondent of William Porcher Miles's provocatively asked the young fire-eater: "Think you that 360,000 Slaveholders will dictate terms for 3,000,000 of non-slaveholders at the South—I fear not, I mistrust our own people more than I fear all of the efforts of the Abolitionists."[3]

Reinforced by a powerful racism, planters had wooed the region's yeomen by combining the prospect of future slave ownership with the incredible notion that black inferiority made all white men equal. That had worked in the Age of Jackson, but might the slaveless soon give a receptive hearing to Republican free-labor doctrines? Would their loyalties shift when Abraham Lincoln began to build a Southern wing to his party as he appointed antislavery men to the post offices of the South and made an antiplanter appeal for the votes of yeomen and white artisans?

Maybe not. Republican opposition to slavery's expansion roused the cotton South's most primal fear, one that helped planters hold the allegiance of those owning no slaves. Filled with anxiety by the predicted doubling of the South's slave population over the next two decades, Southerners wondered what the region might do with so many slaves when soil exhaustion reduced their agricultural productivity. Might large numbers of bondmen become insurrectionary, especially if Republicans flooded the South with abolitionist speakers and antislavery literature? Realistic or not, slaveowners or not, Southern whites generally feared such violence. Anxiety made them ready to believe the worst, like the troubling news coming out of Texas in the summer of 1860. A "general revolt of the slaves, aided by white men of the North in our midst," so a local newspaper claimed, had been planned for August. Though the "Texas Troubles" represented politically inspired falsehood and group hysteria, the story quickly spread throughout the South.[4]

If not insurrection, then Republican government might lead to emancipation, which many thought spelled white social degradation and racial amalgamation. According to Mississippi senator Albert Brown, "The [freed] Negro will . . . insist on being treated as an equal—that he shall go to the white man's table, and the white man to his—that he shall share the white man's bed, and the white man his—that his son shall marry the white man's daughter, and the white man's daughter his son. . . . Then will commence the war of races."[5]

Less incendiary secessionists warned that black freedom meant economic and political disaster. The region's economy would collapse because freedmen would refuse to work or, inconsistently, because they would work, for wages below those paid to white artisans and laborers. If permitted to vote, emancipated blacks could seize political control of the cotton states wherein they comprised a near majority, or more, of the residents. White yeomen might soon find themselves ruled by a truly black Republican Party.

Facing a loss of control over the federal government, anticipating a Republican appeal to poor Southern whites, expecting to be penned up with a hostile black population, leaders of the cotton South took little comfort from their region's prosperity and claimed superiority. "We must become a degraded people," Robert Barnwell warned his cousin, Barnwell Rhett, "unless slavery is upheld as a political institution essential to the preservation of our civilisation and therefore to be . . . defended in the same high strain as liberty itself."[6] Now sharing that dreadful anxiety, many Southerners joined fire-eaters in reacting to Lincoln's election not with confidence in their strengths but with a belligerence born of their fears.

∽ In his study of South Carolina, the first state to leave the Union—and not coincidentally the one with the highest proportion of blacks—historian Steven Channing pointed out that fear of emancipation trumped all other concerns. That fear, and the highest percentage of slaveholding families, united the white population across class and regional lines (see Table 2). With three of every five residents living in slavery (over 80 percent in some coastal districts), both planters and yeomen feared a Republican

Table 2. Southern Slavery in 1860

State/Region (order of secession)	Date of Secession	Total Whites (thousands)	Total Blacks (thousands)	Free Blacks (thousands)	Blacks as % of Total Population	Slaveholding Families as % of White Population
South Carolina	20 Dec	291	412	9.9	59%	49%
Mississippi	9 Jan	354	437	0.1	55%	48%
Florida	10 Jan	78	63	1.0	45%	36%
Alabama	11 Jan	526	438	2.7	45%	35%
Georgia	19 Jan	592	466	3.5	44%	38%
Louisiana	26 Jan	357	350	18.6	50%	32%
Texas	1 Feb	421	183	0.4	30%	29%
Lower South		**2,619**	**2,349**	**36.2**	**47%**	**38%**
Virginia	17 Apr	1,047	549	58.0	34%	26%
Arkansas	6 May	324	111	0.1	26%	19%
Tennessee	7 May	827	283	7.3	25%	24%
North Carolina	20 May	630	362	30.5	36%	29%
Upper South		**2,828**	**1,305**	**95.9**	**32%**	**25%**
Delaware	Union	91	22	19.8	19%	3%
Kentucky	Union	919	236	10.7	20%	23%
Maryland	Union	516	171	84.0	25%	13%
Missouri	Union	1,063	119	3.6	10%	13%
Border South		**2,589**	**548**	**118.1**	**17%**	**16%**
Southern total		**8,036**	**4,202**	**250.2**	**34%**	**26%**

Sources: U.S. Bureau of the Census, *Population of the United States in 1860* (Washington, DC: U.S. Government Printing Office, 1864), n.p.; *Historical Statistics of the United States: Colonial Times to 1970*, 2 vols. (Washington, DC: U.S. Government Printing Office, 1975), series A195–209, 1:24–37; and L. C. Gray, *History of Agriculture in the Southern United States to 1860*, 2 vols. (Washington, DC: Carnegie Institute of Washington, 1933), 1:482.

federal government, which to their minds equated to slave insurrection, black emancipation, or race war, and perhaps in time to all three.[7]

Confident of support for secession within their own borders, South Carolina's fire-eaters believed that they had found in Lincoln's election the spark with which to ignite widespread disunion and not leave their state vulnerable to federal coercion should it again act alone. To ensure that the anticipated Republican victory fed the fires of secession, South Carolina radicals used newspapers, speeches, sermons, and a variety of organizations to convey their message. Within their state and beyond, they warned that Lincoln's election meant antislavery government, abolitionist agents, emancipation, and insurrection. Only secession could save the South.

Psychologically prepared to react to a Republican victory in that predetermined fashion, South Carolinians did not await election results. On October 8, they elected a secessionist-minded state legislature, and Governor William Gist sent his brother to North Carolina and five Deep South states to announce South Carolina's intention to secede if only another state would join it. When the legislature assembled to select presidential electors on November 5, Gist held it in session to await confirmation of Lincoln's victory. Then, sustained by pledges from the governors of Alabama and Mississippi, the legislators set December 6 as the date to elect members of a convention to assemble on the 17th for a consideration of the state's future relation to the federal government.

During the Revolutionary War, Americans had begun the practice of using conventions for definitive resolution of fundamental political issues. In new hands, a medieval English institution became the embodiment of the popular will, distinct from and superior to a legislature, the accepted way for citizens to change or approve new constitutions—and, in 1860, take themselves out of an old one. When the convention's delegates met in Columbia, the governor of Florida and secession-minded commissioners from Alabama and Mississippi arrived to urge them on. Three days later, following a move to Charleston to escape a rumored smallpox epidemic, the convention unanimously voted South Carolina out of the Union.

Why such haste? With President James Buchanan denying that he had authority to coerce a seceded state, prompt action gave South Carolina at least two months to prepare for independence free from federal interference. If a new league of seceded states became established before Lincoln took office, it might deter him from attempting the Union's forceful reconstruction. More to the point, as Barnwell Rhett explained in a letter of November 10, successful revolutions leave no "time for re-action on the part of the people."[8] They must not be given time to think. The decision represented no fire-eater coup, however. The convention had acted unanimously, and South Carolinians, even if panicked, overwhelmingly endorsed its decision.

〜 The Gulf states of Mississippi, Florida, and Alabama—next to South Carolina, those with the highest proportions of blacks—followed the Palmetto State out of the Union between January 9 and 11. After election campaigns of about a month's duration they elected convention delegates between December 20 and 24. Florida's assembled on January 3, and those of Alabama and Mississippi, four days later. All three states had a secessionist governor, but their people lacked South Carolina's virtual unanimity of opinion. Radicals consequently met resistance from their conventions' few unionists and larger groups of cooperationists. Differing over whether to reject secession altogether (as the unionists wished) or to achieve it by joint action (the cooperationists' preference), the two groups united in advocating a Southern convention wherein the slave states would jointly determine the conditions under which they would remain in the Union. If the North rejected their terms, the slave states would withdraw together—a course thought less likely to end in war. To secessionists, however, cooperation meant delays that would erode enthusiasm for disunion and, worse, breed inaction when upper South states favored compromise. There must be no repeat of the Nashville Convention's feeble fumbling.

In his examination of secession in Alabama and Mississippi, historian William Barney described the fire-eaters' call as answered by younger men (small planters, slaveowning farmers, and those hoping to acquire slaves) living in areas new to cotton culture.[9] Often lawyers who acquired land and a few slaves after establishing their legal practice, those men of emerging wealth and status regarded Republican leadership as an obstacle to their prospects. With their ambitions already squeezed by rising prices for slaves and land, they put less at risk by secession and saw in Southern independence hopes for cheaper slaves and new lands in Latin America. Though economically motivated, the new secessionists of Alabama and Mississippi reached across class lines to free farmers and artisans with arguments based upon race: Blacks were inferior. Equality with them was politically and socially unthinkable and sexually abhorrent.

Denying the likelihood of war because of the federal army's small size and anticipating help from Great Britain's aristocrats, secessionists pushed ahead while the pro-Southern Buchanan occupied the White House and before Lincoln could appoint abolitionists to federal offices in their states. Aided by volunteer militia organizations, vigilance committees, newspaper editorials, public rallies, wild exaggerations of slave attacks, and fictional insurrection plots such as the Texas Troubles, secessionists simply overwhelmed citizens already unsettled by years of fire-eater agitation.

Cooperation, the radicals charged, was but a subterfuge for cowardly submission to Northern antislavery. Despite that stigma, joint action by all the slave states appealed to diverse groups: wealthy planters in older plantation districts, businessmen with economic ties reaching beyond their states, slaveowners from counties where plantation agriculture was in decline, and yeoman farmers living in the relatively slave-free mountains. The first two looked to Southern influence in Congress and the Supreme Court to restrain Lincoln should he attempt, despite assurances, to attack slavery in the South. They also believed that secession, unless cooperatively achieved, would end in war, high taxes, authoritarian government, and financial chaos. Economic ties influenced the third group, whose members traded their small cotton crop through Tennessee, believed likely to remain within the Union. The subsistence farmers of the last group, though having voted for John Breckinridge in accord with their Jacksonian traditions, broke with their party over secession. Resentful of planter wealth and power, they hated the low status imposed upon them more than they feared the few blacks living among them, nor had they any intention of fighting a rich man's war.

Despite such divisions, Mississippi's cooperationists did poorly in the state's December 20 elections. They won most of the counties with a majority of small landowners and few slaves, but many of the state's yeomen were too dispersed to affect their counties' delegate selection. In regions where slaveholders comprised more than one-quarter of the population, cooperationists ran well only in the extremely wealthy river counties and among Vicksburg and Natchez businessmen. Elsewhere, secessionists won enough contests to give them a 3-to-1 edge when the convention assembled on January 7.

That majority promptly showed its strength by making a secessionist lawyer-planter the convention's permanent president. Urged on by supporters in the hall's galleries and commissioners sent by disunionist governors, it then easily turned back delaying resolutions calling for a Southern convention, awaiting action by four neighboring states, and a popular referendum on any secession resolution. Either loyal to the will of the majority or intimidated by questions about their loyalty, only fifteen cooperationists voted "no" when the convention approved secession the second day. Fearful of putting their action to the voters, the secessionists, by an extremely close 49-to-43 margin, asserted the convention's authority to remain in session to ratify the Confederate constitution expected from a February meeting of seceded states in Montgomery, Alabama. Mississippians would have little to say about their new government.

The results of Alabama's December 24 election showed the state almost equally divided between yeoman cooperationists in the north and slaveowning secessionists in the south. Had the cooperationists made a better campaign, they might have gained the statewide edge with victories in Mobile and the wealthiest Black Belt counties. Even so, Alabama's unionists put up a fight when the convention assembled on January 7. The secessionist candidate for presiding officer won by only eight votes, and cooperationists defeated a resolution questioning the loyalty of anyone opposing disunion.

Using telegrams about alleged federal attacks on slave states and equally false predictions of Virginia's imminent secession, the secessionists defeated by 53 to 45 two cooperationist resolutions calling for a Southern convention and a popular referendum on secession. On the next day, January 11, the convention approved secession by 61 to 39 when several cooperationists concluded that they must now choose between secession and submission. Unsure of their strength in the countryside, however, secessionists refused to authorize either popular election of their state's delegates to the February gathering in Montgomery or allowing Alabamans to ratify any Confederate constitution emerging from that meeting.

In studying the Florida convention, historian Ralph Wooster found both secessionists and cooperationists across the spectrum of slaveowning, occupation, and wealth. As in Alabama, however, Florida's secessionists and cooperationists divided along regional lines. The northern and western (panhandle) counties favored delay, and easterners advocated immediate disunion. By late 1860, however, little unionism survived in Florida; and after secessionists demonstrated their numerical strength, most cooperationists supported a secession resolution on January 10.[10]

∾ With four states abandoning the Union within three weeks, the momentum for secession had built rapidly. If it could roll through Georgia, whose convention gathered on January 16, it might carry at least the cotton South. The decision by the Empire State of the South was critical for other reasons as well.[11] Within the seven Deep South states, it ranked second only to Texas in size and to South Carolina in date of founding, and it had more people, more slaves, and more slaveholders than any other. Without Georgia's secession, South Carolina might remain physically isolated, and only a narrow 150-mile strip of Florida's panhandle joined that state to Alabama. How could secessionists build a viable confederacy from such scattered fragments? Georgia, moreover, had a history of squelching disunion, as it had when accepting the Compromise of 1850. It might again follow the prompting of favorite sons Alexander Stephens, Robert Toombs, and Howell Cobb, who had then reached across party lines to crush, in the words of Kentucky's senator Henry Clay, "the spirit of discord, disunion and Civil War."[12]

A decade later, however, Toombs and Cobb deserted Stephens, who had also strongly opposed the breakup of the Democratic Party at Charleston and, after rejecting second place on the Douglas ticket, campaigned hard to defeat Breckinridge, who won Georgia by only a plurality of the votes. Failing to elect his friend Stephen Douglas, Stephens was given another opportunity to preserve the Union when the Georgia legislature gathered to consider disunion the day after Lincoln's election.

Secessionist Governor Joseph Brown greeted the legislators with a recommendation to take their state out of the Union without reference to a convention. The legislators, wishing to hear the views of the state's leaders on so vital an issue, invited twenty-two of them to address it. Supported by the presence of such fire-eaters as Barnwell Rhett, Edmund Ruffin, and W. L. Harris of Mississippi, Georgians Robert Toombs and Thomas Cobb, Howell's brother, drew cheers as they boldly endorsed secession. In a spirited, well-reasoned response to their passion, Stephens extolled the Union's advantages, called secession an unworthy response to loss of an election, and maintained that Congress and the Supreme Court would ensure that Lincoln did no harm. Hoping that delay might awaken secession-defeating second thoughts, Stephens pressed the legislature to take the issue to the people by calling for election of a convention to consider Georgia's response to a Republican victory. Swayed by Stephens's address, the legislators chose the path of delay and set January 2 for the election of delegates to a convention convening two weeks later.

Little about his origins suggested that Stephens would achieve such influence. Unlike Toombs and the Cobb brothers, all born to wealth, he was the son of a Georgia farmer of modest means whose own father had fled Scotland for Pennsylvania following the defeat of Bonnie Prince Charlie at Culloden Moor. After serving in the American Revolution, Grandfather Stephens, his wife, and eight children migrated to middle Georgia, where he and his son became yeomen farmers. Orphaned at fourteen, Alexander and his five siblings shared an inheritance of only nine slaves and 230 acres.

In addition to humble beginnings, physical problems conspired to dissuade Stephens from an active public life. Sickly as a child, in adulthood he was plagued with maladies—rheumatoid arthritis, cervical disk disease, colitis, bladder stones, angina, migraine headaches, and pruritis—that filled his life with pain and often left him incapacitated. Known as Little Aleck, though he grew to a not unusual 5' 7", Stephens rarely weighed over ninety pounds and was burdened by an unusually small head, oversized ears, and an ashen complexion. His consequently freakish appearance and ailments may account for two other disabilities, chronic melancholy and frequent depression. Overcoming all obstacles, however, Stephens obtained an education with the aid of Presbyterians hopeful that he would enter the ministry. Finding him a diligent student who excelled at oratory, Franklin College graduated Little Aleck first in his class. Known for his generosity and sensitivity to others, he had by then struck up friendships with classmates Howell Cobb and Herschel Johnson, two future governors—the first also a cabinet member and the second Stephen Douglas's 1860 running mate. After a short period in which he taught school and tutored a planter's children, Stephens abandoned education and returned to Crawfordville, his boyhood home.

The self-taught twenty-two-year-old passed the bar examinations in July 1834 and joined a judicial circuit including Cobb and Toombs, who would become closer to Stephens than anyone other than his brother Linton. Within a year, hard work, oratorical skills, and the ability to read a jury enabled Aleck to earn a good income from the law and begin building an estate eventually worth over $60,000 and including thirty-four slaves. Stephens began his political career in 1837, when he won a seat in the Georgia assembly. Five years later he entered the state senate but left in 1843 when Georgia Whigs sent him to the U.S. Congress following a statewide campaign. Thereafter, he represented his district until his retirement in 1859.

Though occasionally yielding to a hot temper and a sharp tongue, Stephens was a man of principle and no revolutionary. Once his initial anger had subsided, he habitually advocated compromise and sectional forbearance. Seeing no need for slavery to expand, he opposed demanding a territorial cession from Mexico in 1848 and later embraced both Popular Sovereignty and the admission of free California so long as the government did not humiliate the South by denying it satisfaction on other issues. When President Taylor's death and Senator Douglas's skill produced the Compromise of 1850, Stephens considered the South satisfied.

He supported the Kansas-Nebraska Act, even pulling off the parliamentary maneuver that passed the bill through the House, though he doubted that slavery would ever be established in Kansas. Behaving like a radical, Stephens also momentarily put aside his abhorrence of lawlessness to support both filibustering attacks aimed at seizing Cuba and Buchanan's efforts to force the proslavery Lecompton constitution on Kansas, even though that mocked Popular Sovereignty. Soon regretting the dishonesty of that endeavor, Little Aleck suggested what became the 1858 English bill, which, by delaying the admission of Kansas for two years, permitted the South to save face and the new state to be slave free.

Correctly perceiving the Democratic Party as the guardian of Southern interests in Washington and regarding Douglas as sound on slavery, Stephens condemned fire-eater efforts to destroy the party unless it adopted a slave-code platform on which no Northern Democrat could win election. In his view, Southern Democrats betrayed their Northern allies and destroyed their party for nothing: a federal slave code that Stephens's biographer, Thomas Schott, accurately described as protecting "virtually nonexistent property in territories most believed utterly inhospitable to slavery."[13]

More than alleged threats to slavery, the conservative Stephens, like Salmon Chase, feared disorder and anarchy, which the Georgian associated with disunion. He therefore split with Toombs, worked for the election of Douglas, and in the wake of Lincoln's victory successfully urged the Georgia legislature to take the question of secession to the people by means of a convention. Then, incredibly, Stephens gave up. Despite widespread public support for the Union, close contests between two slates of delegates in all but 19 of Georgia's 113 counties, and an Opposition Party press that railed against secession, Little Aleck, except for one brief speech, inexplicably sat out the campaign. Meanwhile, secessionists such as Thomas Cobb crisscrossed the state, giving three and four speeches per day in the villages and crossroads of rural Georgia. Even as a delegate to the closely divided convention, Stephens failed to work with others to devise strategy or propose resolutions. He spoke only once, for a desultory fifteen minutes. Former governor Johnson called his remarks "half-hearted and ineffective," a virtual "surrender of the contest."[14] Had the highly respected Stephens made a vigorous campaign, or had he even taken the lead at the convention, Georgia might have remained within the Union and stalled the rush to secession.

Deceit also helped to promote disunion. Despite heavy, chilling rains that kept many rural unionists at home on Election Day, the results were so close that secessionist Governor Brown withheld them until April 1861 and then submitted a false report indicating a substantial secessionist triumph—50,243 votes to 37,123. Estimating the actual vote as a 42,744-to-41,717 *cooperationist* victory, historian Michael Johnson accounted for Brown's deceit.[15] Even if the county breakdown had given the delegate edge to disunion, an accurate and timely count could well have given secessionists pause even as it inspired their opponents.

Despite gubernatorial dishonesty, the convention's early votes were sufficiently close to suggest that Stephens might have made a difference. The convention rejected the cooperationists' call for a Southern convention by only 164 to 133, and a test vote on a secession ordinance succeeded by a narrow 166-to-130 margin. With no hope of a Southern convention and their choices reduced to secession or submission, many cooperationists gave up. The state's formal resolution of secession passed by a vote of 208 to 89, with Stephens against it.

As with Mississippi and Alabama, opposition to immediate secession had come from counties with few slaves and slaveowners, where farmers emphasized subsistence over commercial agriculture. As the proportion of slaves in a county increased, so did the vote for delegates committed to secession. Town life had a similar effect. Although 53 percent of rural voters opposed secession, 69 percent of urban Georgians favored disunion. Michael Johnson concluded that usually cautious conservatives might have made the difference in the convention when they perceived secession as the best means to guarantee their continued political direction of the state. In confirmation of that analysis, the Georgia convention, after voting the state out of the

Union, remained in session to write a new, less democratic constitution reducing the influence of the state's yeomen.

～〉 With Georgia secure, secession swept through Louisiana and Texas, overcoming otherwise crippling obstacles.[16] Until its legislature met in special session on December 10, Louisiana seemed the most conservative of the Gulf States. Like Georgia, it had rejected secession in 1850, and in the recent presidential election New Orleans had gone 2 to 1 for John Bell over Breckinridge. Though the Southern Democrat had won a statewide plurality, a majority of Louisianans gave their votes to Bell or Douglas, the unionist candidates.

Texans, who had elected a unionist governor and two moderate congressmen in 1859, also appeared solidly within the Union. Secession appealed to immigrants from the Deep South, but they were a majority only in the plantation and cotton society of east Texas. Former Upper South yeoman families producing meat and grain for the U.S. Army dominated north Texas, and in the state's southern counties Germans and Mexicans, both generally indifferent or even hostile to slavery, outnumbered Texans linked to the slave economy. Frontiersmen relying upon the army for protection from Comanches also favored the Union, as did Texans in and around the state capital at Austin. There, Governor Sam Houston, a dedicated Jacksonian and the hero of the state's war for independence, blocked fire-eaters such as editor John Marshall and U.S. Senator Louis Wigfall.

Even so, secessionists captured both states. In Louisiana a vigorous Democratic campaign, reinforced by secession's momentum and recently organized military units and Southern Rights associations, helped delegates favoring immediate disunion amass a total of 20,448 votes to their opponents' 17,296. By the time the state's convention assembled on January 23, the apparent collapse of Washington's efforts to achieve sectional compromise had caused many Bell supporters to reconsider their unionism. Because five Deep South states had already left the Union, cooperationist arguments about the risks of separate state action lost much of their force. New Orleans merchants, initially opposed to secession, now chose handling the Deep South's cotton trade over moving the Midwest's grain shipments.

With many minds changed, the convention's early decisions previewed secession's triumph and revealed how the energy of the secession campaign had demoralized cooperationists. Before voting on disunion, the delegates defeated, by margins of 106 to 24 and 73 to 47, cooperationist resolutions proposing a meeting of the slave states and calling for a popular referendum on secession. On January 25, the convention took Louisiana out of the Union by a vote of 84 to 43 and later concluded its work by appointing delegates to the Montgomery meeting and ordering seizure of over $500,000 in the U.S. Mint and Customs House.

Several factors, some unique to Texas, undermined its alliance of unionists and cooperationists. As elsewhere in the Deep South, the state's rights wing of the Democratic Party had made good use of John Brown's raid to portray all Republicans and most Northerners as abolitionists threatening the state's social stability. Then the army's ineffective response to Comanche attacks on the frontier and a brief Mexican occupation of Brownsville caused affected Texans to question the Union's value. The two-month delay in organizing the House of Representatives in the winter of 1859–60 also prompted fears of a Union in chaos.

After gaining control of the state Democratic Party in the spring of 1860, Texas radicals intensified that sense of crisis when they joined William Yancey's effort to disrupt the national party's convention in Charleston and made of Lincoln's victory a justification for secession. Following the Republican victory, former Whigs in east Texas began to shift their allegiance. Fearful of social disorder, they chose secession, even if it meant war, as less threatening than alleged Republican abolitionism. As in Louisiana, the secession of other states removed much of the fear of separate state action.

When Governor Houston thought to turn back disunion's rising tide by refusing to call the legislature into special session, radicals published an unofficial address calling for election of delegates to a convention meeting on January 28. When that extralegal effort failed to collapse, Houston announced a special session in hopes that the legislature would refuse to recognize the convention. Instead, it approved the assembly, on condition that its work be submitted to a popular referendum. On February 1, by a margin of 166 to 8, the convention sent to the people of Texas its secession resolution, which three-quarters of them approved on February 23. By that date, representatives from the other six Deep South states meeting in Montgomery had formed the Confederate States of America.

∿ Throughout the Deep South respected leaders such as Houston and persuasive orators and skilled parliamentarians such as Stephens had proven themselves unable to halt or even slow the Deep South's rush to disunion. How could that be? In a general way, the answer lies in the existence of a crisis mentality. For decades, fire-eaters had rehearsed Southern grievances and prepared Southern minds to react energetically to every real or imagined slight. The collapse of national political parties, beginning with the Whigs, also facilitated extremism. With that party fatally split along sectional lines and its Southern wing freed of the need to compromise policies with Northern colleagues, Whig candidates made sectional appeals for votes. To counter former Whigs portraying themselves as the better guardians of slavery, Democrats demanded more of their Northern allies, exposing them to defeat and straining party unity. That process made the Democrats virtually a Southern sectional party before radicals destroyed it altogether at Charleston. The party through which the South had long dominated the federal government and restrained an assertive North lay in fragments.

In that superheated political atmosphere, there had also appeared in the mid-1850s a sectional Northern party dedicated to containment of slavery as a means to achieve its ultimate extinction. Aided by John Brown's raid, the South's radicals had little trouble in convincing many Southerners that Republicans were all abolitionists, even insurrectionists, seeking the immediate destruction of slavery and Southern society. The Deep South consequently regarded Lincoln's election with both horror and loathing. To extricate the South from such allegedly dreadful circumstances, fire-eaters proposed one simple, easily understood plan: separate state secession followed by formation of a Southern confederacy.

Their opponents had a harder case to make. Those openly devoted to the Union reminded Southerners of its benefits and warned that secession in response to a constitutional election was both unethical and dangerous. If Democrats, unionists might also urge their fellow citizens to look to rebuilding their shattered party, helping it once again to serve as the guardian of Southern interests. Unionist former Whigs might point out that Lincoln had promised to accept slavery where it existed and that both Congress and the Supreme Court could contain any direct attack on the institution. All such arguments had an unfortunately passive character when compared to fire-eater energy and the supposed dimensions of the crisis.

Attempting to relieve Southern anxiety by offering stronger action, cooperationists proposed that the slave states meet in convention to devise concessions that the North must accept lest a united South leave the Union. Lacking secession's deceptive clarity, that proposal produced little agreement on details and left too many questions unanswered. Where and when would this convention meet? What would it demand of the North? What if the upper South favored a compromise that the cotton states could not accept? Barring that, by what method would the South determine the North's acceptance of its ultimatum? If the convention failed to achieve intersectional compromise, should the South secede immediately or wait until the Republican president had committed some "overt act" hostile to slavery? And might not division and delay from such a complex process destroy the impulse for secession? Though not a balanced description of the antagonists' positions, the Hayneville (Alabama) *Chronicle* understood the situation. Two days after Lincoln's election it predicted that "two parties will take the field, one for action, prompt and efficient; the other to eulogise the glories of the Union, and preach submission to the sway of Black Republicanism."[17]

With the public drawn by secession's decisiveness, selling an ill-defined convention scheme demanded both solid organization and political stamina. Deep South unionists and cooperationists typically lacked both. Whereas the secessionists possessed the local Democratic political apparatus seized at the time of the Breckinridge nomination, their opponents lacked a party organization with which to devise strategy, dispatch speakers, and mount campaigns for election of delegates opposing immediate secession. Because many unionist voters lived in the less accessible parts of the rural Deep South, the lack of organization and speakers with which to reach them seriously weakened the cooperationist cause. Fire-eater-inspired vigilance committees, volunteer military companies, secessionist governors, and even clergymen working against secession's opponents only made the task more daunting.

Suspecting the struggle already lost, secession's opponents grew demoralized, made feeble efforts to oppose disunion, or joined Stephens in sitting out the campaign. Like him, many of them simply gave up. His brother Linton lamented Stephens's despair and urged him to action: "You can save the country, I do firmly believe." Stephens could not be moved. He apprehended that "no power can prevent [secession]. Our destiny seems to be fixed." Convinced that "the State will secede," Georgia's leading unionist decided to do no more than "maintain my principles to the last."[18] Such inactivity wins no political wars, especially in a crisis pushed forward by a powerful momentum and resting on decades of agitation.

NOTES

1. Stephens to J. Henly Smith, July 10, 1860, reprinted in Ulrich B. Phillips, ed., *The Correspondence of Robert Toombs, Alexander H. Stephens, and Howell Cobb*, vol. 2, *Annual Report of the American Historical Association for 1911* (Washington, DC: American Historical Association, 1913), 487.

2. For the economic condition of the cotton South on the eve of secession as summarized in this section of the chapter see Roger L. Ransom, *Conflict and Compromise: The Political Economy of Slavery, Emancipation, and the American Civil War* (Cambridge, UK: Cambridge University Press, 1989), 41–81, and William L. Barney, *The Secessionist Impulse: Alabama and Mississippi in 1860* (Princeton, NJ: Princeton University Press, 1974), 3–26.

3. Daniel Hammond quoted in Steven A. Channing, *Crisis of Fear: Secession in South Carolina* (New York: W. W. Norton, 1970), 256.

4. Pro-Breckinridge editor Charles Pryor quoted in Walter L. Buenger, *Secession and the Union in Texas* (Austin: University of Texas Press, 1984), 56.

5. Brown quoted in John McCardell, *The Idea of a Southern Nation: Southern Nationalists and Southern Nationalism, 1830–1860* (New York: W. W. Norton, 1979), 323–24.

6. Barnwell quoted in Channing, *Crisis of Fear*, 66.

7. Channing's *Crisis of Fear* is the basis of this section's description of secession in South Carolina.

8. Rhett quoted in ibid., 248.

9. For this section's description of secession in Alabama and Mississippi see Barney, *Secessionist Impulse.*

10. Ralph A. Wooster, *The Secession Conventions of the South* (Princeton, NJ: Princeton University Press, 1962), 67–79.

11. In addition to Schott's biography of Stephens (see note 12), this section's description of secession in Georgia draws upon Michael P. Johnson, *Toward a Patriarchal Republic: The Secession of Georgia* (Baton Rouge: Louisiana State University Press, 1977).

12. Clay quoted in Thomas E. Schott, *Alexander H. Stephens of Georgia: A Biography* (Baton Rouge: Louisiana State University Press, 1988), 129. Schott's biography is the basis of the sketch of Stephens in the remainder of this chapter.

13. Ibid., 292.

14. Johnson quoted in ibid., 321.

15. Johnson, *Patriarchal Republic,* 63–64.

16. This section on Louisiana and Texas follows Wooster, *Secession Conventions,* 101–35; Willie M. Caskey, *Secession and Restoration of Louisiana,* Louisiana State University Studies no. 36 (Baton Rouge: Louisiana State University Press, 1938), 1–44; and Buenger, *Secession in Texas.*

17. *Chronicle* quoted in Barney, *Secessionist Impulse,* 231.

18. Linton Stephens and Alexander Stephens quoted in Schott, *Stephens,* 305, 312, and 319. See also page 316.

CHAPTER SEVEN

JEFFERSON DAVIS AND THE FORMATION OF THE COTTON CONFEDERACY

We have pulled a temple down that has been
built three-quarters of a century. We must clear
the rubbish away to reconstruct another.
—Andrew Calhoun[1]

If without cause they destroy the present Govt.,
the best in the world, what hopes would
I have that they would not bring untold
hardships upon the people in their efforts
to give us one of their modelling?
—Alexander Stephens[2]

HAVING TAKEN SEVEN weeks to fracture the Union, delegates from the seceded states required only an afternoon's conversation to plan their new confederacy. On February 3, 1861, fortified by lunch and meeting informally in the lobby of the Exchange, Montgomery's most prestigious hotel, about twenty of the first delegates to arrive reached consensus on the "Georgia Plan," which proposed what should be done when the convention opened at noon the next day. Despite some objections, the Exchange conferees agreed to act boldly. Though sent to Alabama's capital to draft a constitution, they would defer that task and, usurping authority not given, establish a government. They would declare themselves legislators, choose a president, and create executive departments. Constituting only one-half of the delegates en route to Montgomery, they were determined to convince later arrivals to join them in doing no less. Preparation of a permanent constitution, its ratification by the states, and popular elections to fill its offices could wait. In the meantime, a provisional government would write laws, make decisions, and implement policies.[3]

Holding to his principles and fueled by his ambition, fire-eating Barnwell Rhett roundly condemned the Georgia Plan. In his opinion, making a congress of the convention and using it to pick a president ran roughshod over state sovereignty. If the convention did so, "we will only have changed masters,"[4] replacing Washington's tyrannical government with another in Montgomery. Hoping to become the father of his country as well as the father of secession, Rhett also resented the influence of Georgia's three delegates of presidential caliber—Howell Cobb, Robert Toombs, and Alexander Stephens.

Despite Rhett's reservations, the delegates had good reasons for their extralegal actions. They saw great risks in limiting themselves to drafting a permanent constitution that the states must ratify before proceeding to election of legislators and a president. That course would leave the seceded states without "national" government for no less than a month, by which time Abraham Lincoln would occupy the White House and might have begun forcible reconstruction of the Union. To prevent that, the seceded states had immediate need of a government that could raise money, create armed forces, seek foreign recognition, and negotiate their peaceful separation from the Union. Creating a new government by fiat had a second advantage. It deferred the popular elections feared by delegates from Georgia and Alabama because of both states' large unionist populations. What if secession's opponents in those states—or others—shattered the cotton states' tenuous unity by rejecting a new constitution or electing a unionist president and legislative majority? Was it not safer to consult the popular will only when citizens could be trusted to render an electoral judgment that would not shatter a new government?

With thirty-seven delegates present when William Chilton, leader of the host Alabama delegation, called it to order on February 4, the convention lacked only six of its accredited members. Of the whole number, the mostly middle-aged body included thirty-three lawyers, some also among its seventeen planters; thirty-nine had the equivalent of a college education, and all but eight owned slaves. The fact that just two members had never held high public office attested to the group's capacities. At least twenty were life-long Democrats, and six had been Whigs. Others had supported the variety of political factions active in the South as the old parties fractured in the 1850s.

Oddly, only twenty-four of the delegates had advocated disunion prior to their state's secession. Among that radical two dozen, Alexander Stephens expected to find all the convention's "selfish, ambitious, and unscrupulous."[5] If so, he might keep company with its nineteen former cooperationists and unionists—an indication of the extent to which the seceded states had already rejected fire-eater leadership and turned toward moderate men.

With many delegates committed to the Georgia Plan, the first day's session went as planned. Rhett's cousin, Robert Barnwell, became acting president and, after the invocation, presided over the selection of a temporary secretary, verification of each delegate's credentials, and the election of Howell Cobb as permanent presiding officer. Reflecting understandings reached at the Exchange, Cobb urged the convention to "assume all responsibility which may be necessary for the successful completion of the great work committed to our care."[6] After the election of a permanent secretary and minor officers, Stephens proposed the creation of rules to govern the body's deliberations, and for that purpose Cobb appointed him to chair a committee of five. The meeting, which had impressed observers with its harmony and smooth efficiency, then adjourned to await the committee's recommendations.

Indicative of what Stephens and his committee hoped that the Montgomery convention might become, they wrote "Congress" into the rules that they proposed to the convention the next afternoon. Stephens's strange appearance had previously caused some delegates to doubt his abilities, but as they studied his committee's handiwork and listened to his skillful defense of its proposed rules, they quickly began to admire his intellect. With the rules approved, South Carolina's Christopher Memminger rose, as planned, to move creation of a Committee of Twelve. That body, he explained, should frame a provisional constitution to convert the convention into a legislature and provide for selection of a provisional president. Drafting a permanent constitution for submission to the states would follow establishment of a working government. When some objected to the convention's seizing powers not given, other delegates promptly put the body into secret session, avoiding any public squabble as they devised a resolution reflecting the spirit of Memminger's motion.

For the next three days, while the Committee of Twelve (two delegates from each state) labored and the printer set type, the convention met only briefly. Under Memminger's leadership, the committee's members met full-time, starting after dinner on the day of its creation, when they agreed to use the U.S. Constitution as a model but eliminate such provisions as seemed inapplicable to the functions of a convention-become-congress. On the next day the seven Democrats and five former Whigs got down to details. With the Montgomery delegates already forming a unicameral body, the committee members eliminated portions of the U.S. Constitution concerning congressional organization and elections. They retained, however, congressional authority to enact laws, raise revenue, and declare war. In keeping with Southern orthodoxy, they modified the necessary-and-proper clause and controversial provisions on taxation, tariffs, and transportation improvements. Continuing the ban on the African slave trade, the committee also hoped to coerce slave-exporting states of the upper South into the Confederacy by a further prohibition of slave imports from slave states remaining within the Union.

After appending to their draft the existing eleven amendments of the U.S. Constitution, the committee gave to their Provisional Congress, voting by states, authority to elect a president and vice president. To maintain the president's subordination to the legislature, the draft proposed that the Congress might, by two-thirds vote and for any reason, remove him from office and appoint a temporary president. The draft made a Supreme Court of the district court justices (one for each state) but permitted them to assemble as the nation's highest court only with congressional approval. After strengthening fugitive slave provisions of the U.S. Constitution along the lines of the Compromise of 1850 and giving two-thirds of the Provisional Congress authority to amend the temporary constitution—at any time and without reference to the states—the committee proposed Montgomery as the new nation's capital.

The convention expected to devote its fourth session, the next day, to a debate of the committee's draft. Because the printer had been unable to complete his task, Memminger instead read aloud from a handwritten copy of the "Constitution for the Provisional Government of the Confederate States of North America." The convention then adjourned until all the delegates had time to receive and study the document more fully.

When the convention assembled for its fifth session on February 8, each delegate's desk held a printed copy of the proposed provisional constitution. Stephens began the amendments when he proposed elimination of "North" from the title of the new nation, making it the Confederate States of America—a change appealing to Southerners who expected that their slave empire would soon include Cuba, northern Mexico, and other parts of Latin America. Taking up the principal issue, the convention rejected amendments, favored only by Mississippi and Florida, designed to deny it legislative authority and prevent it from becoming a working government. Minor changes then followed. The president was given a line-item veto, tariff provisions were altered to facilitate free trade, and the legislature received authority to admit new states. For the most part, however, the delegates turned aside objections to the draft. At midnight, following a nine-hour session, the delegations of six states—Texans had yet to vote on secession—gave the provisional constitution their unanimous approval.

The Provisional Congress created that night did not complete a permanent constitution until March 11, a month later, and the last of the Deep South states ratified it on April 22, ten days after the assault on Fort Sumter. In accord with that document, election of a permanent government took place only in the fall of 1861, with its constitutional legislators and president taking office in early 1862. For the selection of those who would lead their nation during that long interregnum, the Montgomery delegates set the afternoon of February 9.

~~~ Rhett and Alabama's fire-eating William Yancey, whatever their hopes, never figured importantly in the contest for the presidency. Their selection would have given the Confederacy a reputation for extremism likely to keep the upper South in the Union.

Besides, few delegates considered either man a competent administrator or leader. The choice would be made from more moderate, even conservative, men: Jefferson Davis of Mississippi and the three Georgians—Howell Cobb, Stephens, and Toombs.

Cobb, however, had little chance, even though he was constantly pumped for by his brother Tom, also a delegate from Georgia, and many delegates believed that the Empire State of the South deserved the presidency. His support for the Compromise of 1850 and subsequent speedy return to the Democratic Party caused radicals to regard Cobb as a man of great ambition but little principle. The merchants of Louisiana also had faint regard for the indifferent service that he had rendered as James Buchanan's treasury secretary.

A man of principle, intelligent, and with good political skills, the gregarious Toombs let alcohol spoil his chances. Though a big man, even a few drinks powerfully affected him, and many delegates had begun to notice. On the third evening of the convention, Toombs had drunk deeply during a dinner with his friend Stephens before going on to a party given for all the delegates by South Carolina's James and Mary Chesnut. By the evening's end, his colleagues judged Toombs unsuitable, a man lacking in self-control and therefore dangerously unfit to lead their new nation.

Stephens, by contrast, rose steadily in the estimation of the delegates. An opponent of secession until the end, he nonetheless won the respect of radicals by his adherence to principle. Having also impressed the delegates with his intelligence, mastery of parliamentary rules, and contributions to the provisional constitution, even fire-eaters such as South Carolina's Lawrence Keitt and Texas's Louis Wigfall thought to make him president. It hurt Stephens's chances that, unlike the insincere Cobb, he genuinely professed no desire for high office. When, during the debate over the provisional constitution, Stephens turned down Keitt's offer of South Carolina's support, that important delegation looked elsewhere. There, taking cuttings in his rose garden at Brierfield, within a bend of the Mississippi River, and hoping to serve as the new confederacy's general in chief, stood Jefferson Davis.

For some time that preference had undermined the Mississippi delegation's advocacy of Davis. At least it did so until the last member to arrive, Alexander Clayton, brought with him a letter in which Davis, after making the obligatory protest against election, agreed to serve the Confederacy in any way that his new countrymen might demand. Because the provisional constitution made its chief executive both president and commander in chief, would not "President" Davis also have his wish?

During the evening of February 8 all but the Georgia delegation met to determine how they would vote when Congress convened at noon the next day. Each state had one vote, with four required for election. Further complicating the election was a widespread desire that it be unanimous and the requirement that each state's vote be determined by a majority of its delegates. Without a majority for a single candidate, the state lost its vote. Within those limits, the delegations sifted the possibilities. Always dreading that secession must end in war, Stephens undercut his remaining supporters by acknowledging his reluctance to strike the first violent blow in any confrontation with the Union.[7] By circulating the falsehood that Georgia had settled on Howell Cobb and expected to see him elected, Tom Cobb destroyed whatever small chance his brother may have had. Barnwell and James Chesnut finally brought South Carolina behind Davis, which gave the Mississippian the vote of Florida as well. Alabama reluctantly rejected Yancey as too extreme and Toombs for his drinking, and Tom Cobb's lies helped put the state behind Davis, as did the belief that Virginia favored him. When Louisiana heard from Tom Cobb, it abandoned Stephens for Davis, a neighbor who understood the needs of the riverine states as no Georgian ever could.

When the Georgians met the next morning, they prepared to give their vote to Toombs until Tom Cobb announced that several states now supported Davis. To verify that claim, the Georgians sent Martin Crawford to canvass the other delegations. Before he left, Toombs proposed that if the other five had indeed gone for Davis, Crawford should ask the vice presidency for Stephens so that Georgia might receive something. Little Aleck agreed; so did the other delegations.

Later that afternoon, the delegates walked to the Alabama statehouse, their temporary home, and came forward, by states, to take their oaths of office under the provisional constitution and begin the process of creating standing legislative committees.

Concluding the day's work, they elected Jefferson Davis and Alexander Stephens provisional president and vice president of the Confederate States of America. Ignoring their state convention's instructions, acting in some secrecy and considerable haste, and failing to consult their fellow citizens, a handful of state's rights proponents had selected those men who were about to lead several million people standing on the brink of war.

∼ Who was this man picked to govern the new nation? More than one colleague thought that he looked the part—"tall, slender, with a soldierly bearing, a fine head, an intellectual face." He had "a look of culture and refinement about him that made a favorable impression from the first."[8] For a nation facing the prospect of war, Davis also had an impressive résumé. A West Pointer, six years a lieutenant in the regular army, the heroic commander of a Mexican War volunteer regiment, and Franklin Pierce's highly regarded secretary of war, Davis seemed the ideal war leader. His political credentials were almost as impressive: one term in the House of Representatives before resigning to take command of the First Mississippi Volunteers, two terms in the U.S. Senate interrupted by an unsuccessful campaign for governor, and service in the cabinet.

Davis's family background—great-grandson of a Welsh immigrant who became a Philadelphia drayman and innkeeper—would not have impressed the South's first families, but it did him no harm among westerners. His grandfather, the youngest of six children, had gone south, to South Carolina and Georgia, where he died shortly before the birth of Samuel Emory Davis, Jefferson's elderly, severe, undemonstrative, and ultimately bankrupt father. The tenth child of parents constantly on the move, the future Confederate president was born in a Kentucky log cabin with fewer than a hundred miles and nine months separating him from Abraham Lincoln, another son of itinerant Southern parents. Two years later, Samuel twice had the family on the move again before ultimately settling in a planter's cottage in Woodville, Mississippi.

Educated above the norm at a variety of schools in Mississippi and Kentucky, young Davis had thought to become a lawyer, like Joseph, his domineering older brother. When their father failed financially and soon died, Joseph, twenty-three-years' Jefferson's senior, pressed his indecisive younger brother to enter West Point, which graduated him in 1828. When Davis left the regular army, Joseph once again shaped his future. With the use of eight hundred acres and a loan to buy ten slaves, the former lieutenant began growing cotton and in time became master of a plantation, a grand mansion, and more than six dozen slaves. His membership in the cotton elite must have reassured the slave-owners who made Davis their president.

Though never sufficiently radical to satisfy fire-eaters such as Rhett, Davis's speeches, actions, and votes in the dozen years before 1861 had given him the mantle of John Calhoun and placed him near the forefront of the secession movement. Before 1848 he had adopted the proslavery argument and defended slavery as divinely ordained, a benefit to both Africans and Southern civilization. Nor, he believed, must slavery be denied access to the territories; doing so would soon make of the South a permanent minority within the nation. Spreading slavery, he artfully claimed, would ensure the "moral and intellectual progress of the slave" and promote his emancipation.[9]

Whatever the validity of that rumination, Davis's politics seemed sound. A strict constructionist opposed to protective tariffs, national banks, and federally financed interstate transportation projects, he advocated territorial expansion but threatened disunion if faced with legislation hostile to Southern interests. In 1848 he had condemned David Wilmot's effort to bar slavery from the Mexican Cession and proposed instead to guarantee a place for it there by an extension of the Missouri Compromise line. In that debate, Davis took a position akin to Yancey's when he warned Northern Democrats that the South, "under the necessity for self-preservation,"[10] must leave their party if Northerners refused to join in defense of Southern interests.

Davis also stood with radicals in condemning the Compromise of 1850. Supporting fire-eating Governor John Quitman's call for a special session of the Mississippi legislature, Davis claimed that "the South would be infinitely benefitted by a dissolution of the Union." In that year, however, only South Carolina, Georgia, and Mississippi even called conventions. Their failure to act did not deter Davis, who warned that if the North

continued to oppose slavery's expansion, "the days of the Confederation [that is, the Union] are numbered." The slave states
must respond with "a compact and a union that will afford protection to their liberties and rights."[11]

With the Senate stalled and time running out on the Kansas-
Nebraska bill, Davis joined with Stephen Douglas, John Breckinridge, and Missouri Senator David Atchison, a school friend, to
convince President Pierce to make its passage an administration
measure. Party discipline and Davis's lobbying of Democrats may
have provided the act's margin of victory in the House. Not surprisingly, then, he later supported efforts to press the Lecompton
constitution on antislavery Kansans. Majority rule had mattered
in the Age of Jackson when the South had held the upper hand,
but no longer. Nor did a sense of proportion. When Congressman Preston Brooks savagely beat Charles Sumner in response
to the Massachusetts senator's insulting speech, Davis called
Brooks's brutal surprise attack on an unarmed man an honorable
response to a "libellous assault upon the reputation" of South
Carolina.[12]

With an eye to eventual Southern independence, Davis also
increasingly supported an economic program similar to that of
fire-eating editor James De Bow. The South must encourage im-
migration from abroad, expand its railroads, build factories, and
strengthen its defenses. Like De Bow, Davis later tossed aside
such preconditions and joined South Carolina's James Hammond
in asserting that King Cotton alone made the South invincible.

By the late 1850s, Davis's public advocacy of disunion seemed
unqualified, and he called himself "a pretty good secessionist."
Though often extolling "the splendid future of an Independent
South," he probably confused cheering Mississippians when he
advised them to respond to a Republican victory in 1860 by both
leaving the Union and making certain that an "Abolitionist President" never took "his seat in the Presidential Chair."[13]

Radicals had reason, however, to question Davis's commitment. At heart a moderate—or suffering habitual indecision?—
Davis wished to secure Southern interests and defeat Republicans
by preserving the Democratic Party. He had consequently urged
the Mississippi delegation not to bolt the Charleston convention
and proposed in the Senate a set of resolutions that might serve

as the platform of a united party. Following the Baltimore meetings he made a vain effort to get John Bell and both Democratic candidates to withdraw in order to unite Lincoln's opponents behind a single compromise candidate. Failing that, he took little further part in the 1860 campaign. When asked the "Norfolk Questions" previously put to Stephen Douglas, Davis dodged them and took what would later become a cooperationist stance: if Lincoln violated the Constitution in ways harmful to the South, then the slave states should convene and seek remedies. Only in early January 1861 did he abandon moderation, advocate immediate and separate state secession, and join with other senators in calling for a convention to meet at Montgomery.

Most members of the Provisional Congress had little objection to a politician's past moderation, although some knowledge of items not found on their new president's résumé might have given them pause. Like his future vice president, Davis suffered from appallingly bad health. Stress or extended exposure to heat and light brought on eruptions of a herpes simplex infection in his left eye, which caused painful facial neuralgia, ulcerated his cornea, and produced a cloudy film that virtually blinded him. The malaria that had struck Davis and killed his first wife, Sarah "Knoxie" Taylor, Zachary Taylor's daughter, also recurred frequently and, like his eye problems, left him temporarily incapacitated. By comparison, Toombs's overindulgence might have struck informed delegates as the lesser danger.

Nor did most delegates suspect that, as war secretary, Davis had "exhibited all the signs of an insecure administrator who, fearing that some detail or other may get the better of him," wrote his biographer, "chooses instead to immerse himself in that detail and thus enslaves himself."[14] By working himself to the point of illness and exhaustion, Davis had kept on top of a small War Department in time of peace. How might he fare as president of a nation at war?

Though Davis gave evidence aplenty to those who knew him well, few in Montgomery would have known of another serious personality flaw. In the opinion of his insightful second wife, Varina Howell, her husband "would not succeed" as a "party manager" because he "did not know the arts of the politician and would not practice them if understood." Witty, open, and generous with a few close friends and those of unquestionably lower social station—children, women, and slaves—Davis could not consistently relate well to the strong-willed men who were his peers. From his days at West Point, he had demonstrated a self-righteous streak and made unreasoning efforts to prove himself free of error. If challenged, he defended himself by splitting hairs and shading the truth. He regularly overreacted to criticism, however slight, with malicious assaults on the character and motives of his accuser. On at least a half-dozen occasions, each in response to a petty quarrel, Davis demonstrated so little self-control that only the intervention of friends kept him out of duels. As he confessed to Varina, "I cannot bear to be suspected or complained of, or misconstrued after explanation."[15]

With self-appointed legislators whose authority rested on an unratified constitution that they feared voters might not approve and led by a deeply flawed but nevertheless zealous and diligent president, the new Southern confederacy set out to pacify or overcome the Union it had just abandoned. In Washington, other men searched for a compromise that might prevent secession in the upper South and provide a basis for reconstructing the Union.

NOTES

1. Andrew Calhoun, John Calhoun's son, to the South Carolina secession convention, December 20, 1860, quoted in William C. Davis, "A Government of Our Own": The Making of the Confederacy (New York: Free Press, 1994), v.

2. Stephens to J. Henly Smith, July 10, 1860, reprinted in Ulrich B. Phillips, ed., The Correspondence of Robert Toombs, Alexander H. Stephens, and Howell Cobb, vol. 2, Annual Report of the American Historical Association for 1911 (Washington, DC: American Historical Association, 1913), 487.

3. On the formation of the Confederate government as described in this chapter see Davis, Government of Our Own.

4. Rhett quoted in ibid., 70.

5. Stephens quoted in ibid., 52.

6. Cobb quoted in ibid., 76.

7. See Thomas E. Schott, Alexander H. Stephens of Georgia: A Biography (Baton Rouge: Louisiana State University Press, 1988), 325–28.

8. Congressman Henry Hilliard as quoted by William C. Davis in his Jefferson Davis: The Man and His Hour (New York: HarperCollins, 1991), 118, which is also the source of this chapter's interpretation of the Confederate president.

9. Davis quoted in ibid., 180.
10. Davis quoted in ibid., 166.
11. Davis quoted in ibid., 182, 200, and 207.
12. Davis quoted in ibid., 252.
13. Davis quoted in ibid., 256, 259, and 268.
14. Ibid., 119.
15. Varina Davis and Jefferson Davis quoted in ibid., 297 and 169.

PART THREE

THE ROAD TO WAR

Both parties deprecated war, but one of them
would *make* war rather than let the nation survive,
and the other would *accept* war rather than
let it perish, and the war came.
—Abraham Lincoln*

ALTHOUGH AN ELECTED government of the Confederacy would not take office for another year, its self-selected leaders showed little reluctance to shape the nation's future. Having no interest in the Union's reconstruction, they shunned the Washington Peace Conference and its effort to gain approval for the compromise proposed by Kentucky senator John Crittenden. Hoping to avoid war, if that could be done without surrender, they sent commissioners to Washington in hopes that President Abraham Lincoln would negotiate a peaceful division of the Union. Meanwhile, they strengthened their new nation's armed forces and prepared to initiate hostilities with attacks on Forts Sumter and Pickens should Lincoln not yield. Concerned for the viability of a seven-state Confederacy, they also encouraged upper South governors such as Virginia's John Letcher to lead their states out of the Union. In that effort, however, they met strong opposition from upper South unionists such as Tennessee senator Andrew Johnson.

For their part, congressional Republicans defended their party's platform while offering compromises insufficient to ensure the continued loyalty of all the upper South, let alone the return of the seven seceded states. In office, Lincoln played for

*From Lincoln's second inaugural address, his emphasis, reprinted in James D. Richardson, ed., *A Compilation of the Messages and Papers of the Presidents, 1789–1897*, 10 vols. (Washington, DC: By Authority of Congress, 1899), 6:276.

time, seeking a peaceful reconstruction of the Union by preventing further secession and undermining support for the Confederacy by limiting its sovereignty, principally by holding the forts within its claimed borders.

CHAPTER EIGHT

JOHN CRITTENDEN AND THE FAILURE OF COMPROMISE

There is no compromise that the seceded States
would accept. There is not a single member of
our [Confederate States] Congress in favor
of reconstruction upon any terms.
—Howell Cobb[1]

WHILE THE DEEP SOUTH states left the Union and founded a new
nation, Washington attempted to limit secession, keep the peace,
and reconstruct the fractured Union. In that effort, President
Buchanan, both houses of Congress, and a national peace conference vainly pursued sectional compromise. They may never have
had a chance. The four-month interregnum between the election
and Abraham Lincoln's inauguration provided time for negotiation, but with Buchanan discredited, congressional Republicans
without policy, and Lincoln in Illinois, the government lacked
leadership. Though ignoring Buchanan's suggestions, the legislators, as in 1820 and 1850, tried to fashion another sectional agreement, but Congress soon discovered that many of its members
refused to be appeased. Nor did the Peace Conference find in the
proposals of Kentucky senator John Crittenden a way to turn the
nation off the path toward destruction.

Before Congress reassembled on December 3, Buchanan and
his cabinet began searching for answers to the questions that
impending disunion posed for the Chief Executive.[2] How might
secession be prevented? Was it even legal? If not, how might
the president fulfill his obligations to protect federal property
and faithfully execute the laws within any seceding state? And
did the Constitution give him—or Congress—authority to resist
secession with armed force? The deeply divided administration

also spent much of November debating the wisdom of an immediate presidential proclamation addressing those questions before, in the end, deferring a response to the president's annual
message to Congress. Meanwhile, the status of the forts and other
federal property within the Deep South intruded on the cabinet's
deliberations.

General in Chief Winfield Scott's disregarded pre-election ad-
vice to strengthen garrisons at nine Southern ports soon acquired
new urgency. On Election Day a Charleston mob had blocked an
attempt by the harbor garrison, located in Fort Moultrie, to move
arms and ammunition from the city's federal arsenal to the fort.
Believing that he had a clear duty to protect federal property,
Buchanan could no longer safely delay a potentially explosive
decision about reinforcements. As he considered what to do about
Charleston Harbor, the president faced a dilemma. Sending reinforcements, as requested by the garrison commander, Colonel
John Gardner, might provoke a violent response, thus hastening
secession in Carolina and beyond. Failing to send them, however, might encourage conflict if a Charleston mob attacked the
harbor garrison in Fort Moultrie, an obsolete bastion largely undefended on its landward side, or violently seized any of the
harbor's other, minimally occupied federal installations. (See frontispiece.) Losing any of them would further dishonor an already
discredited administration.

With three decisions, Buchanan hoped to resolve his dilemma
without encouraging secession. On November 9, he sent Colonel
Benjamin Huger, a Charlestonian, to superintend the arsenal.
Though rejecting reinforcement of the eighty-man harbor garrison lest that bring South Carolina to a boil, the president replaced
its elderly Boston-born commander with the energetic Major Robert Anderson, from the slave state of Kentucky. Before the end of
the month, Buchanan also reached an understanding of sorts with
South Carolina governor William Gist. The president would ignore requests for troops, while the governor would guarantee
the safety of federal property.

In his fourth annual address, the president dealt with the remaining questions. Intended as an appeal for the Union, his message resolved nothing and instead provoked widespread anger.
To the "long-continued and intemperate interference of the North-

ern people with the question of slavery in the Southern States," he assigned sole responsibility for the crisis. Twenty-five years of such "agitation" had fed disunion by afflicting Southerners with "apprehensions of servile insurrection." Unless Northerners stopped their criticism, secession would "become inevitable."[3]

Having rebuked the North, the president challenged Southern dogma by denying that "the Federal Government is a mere voluntary association of States, to be dissolved at pleasure by any one of the contracting parties." A unilateral attempt to break the Union consequently constituted a revolutionary attempt to destroy "the noblest system of government ever devised." Only an unconstitutional act of a "deliberate, palpable, and dangerous" character—not mere loss of an election—could justify disunion.

If the slave states nevertheless proceeded to secession, what recourse had the federal government? The president claimed authority to do no more than protect federal property and faithfully execute federal law. That apparently meant no more than holding the forts, delivering the mail, and collecting customs duties from ships lying outside Southern harbors. Beyond that, "the Executive had no authority to decide what shall be the relations between the Federal Government" and a seceded state. Nor did the Constitution grant to either Congress or the president "the power to coerce a State into submission which is attempting to withdraw or has actually withdrawn from the Confederacy [that is, the Union]."

Having satisfied few men other than himself by declaring secession an illegal act that the government might not punish, Buchanan looked to Congress or a national convention to preserve the Union by adopting the slave-code platform on which John Breckinridge had just failed of election. By amendment, the Constitution should be made to recognize "a right of property in slaves in the States where it now exists or may hereafter exist" and to protect that right in the territories until such time as they applied for statehood. It must, finally, declare "null and void" all state laws impeding a master's right to recover a fugitive slave. After thrusting onto others the ultimate responsibility for resolving the crisis, Buchanan focused on avoiding war—at least until March 4, when the problem would become Lincoln's. To that end, he respected his understanding with Governor Gist by rejecting Major Anderson's request for troops.

Unanticipated events soon proved, however, that the president was not home free. When Secretary of War John Floyd dispatched Major Don Carlos Buell to investigate the situation in Charleston, he carried instructions with momentous consequences. Though offering no reinforcement, Buell advised Anderson that he might concentrate his tiny command at whichever of the harbor's forts "you deem most proper to increase its power of resistance." That surely meant recently completed Fort Sumter, over three miles from the city and entirely occupying a man-made island near the mouth of the harbor. There was a condition, however. Anderson might do so only in the event of "tangible evidence of a design to proceed to a hostile act" against his garrison. Lest his import be missed, the departing Buell obliquely urged that Anderson "not allow the opportunity to escape."[4]

Three days after South Carolina's December 20 secession, a cabinet directive signed by Secretary Floyd appeared to validate Buell's instructions when it ordered Anderson to "exercise sound military discretion" and avoid any "useless sacrifice" in defense of the harbor's forts. Regarding South Carolina's secession as a threat to his command, Anderson used his discretion on the night of December 26 and moved his men to relative safety in Fort Sumter. Outraging Charlestonians and causing their governor to charge bad faith, the move bought Buchanan time by delaying for some months the possibility of effective assault. South Carolina had to content itself with seizing the other, now undefended forts as well as Charleston's federal post office, arsenal, and customs house.[5]

With Anderson's command for the moment secure in the very heart of secession, Fort Sumter assumed great symbolic importance. Should he be driven out, it would be no impromptu act of a Charleston mob but the considered decision of a Southern government. Hoping to keep the peace by putting his garrison beyond easy assault, Anderson had set the stage on which war would begin in mid-April. It might have come sooner.

Another of the forts still in federal hands, Fort Pickens on Santa Rosa Island off the coast of Pensacola, Florida, also demanded the president's attention. Inspired by events in South

Carolina, secessionists seized the Pensacola Navy Yard in January 1861, forcing the army garrison commanded by Lieutenant A. J. Slemmer to seek the watery security of Pickens. To his aid on the 24th, Buchanan sent the warship *Brooklyn* with provisions, military stores, and an artillery company. To preclude Pickens's reinforcement, Florida senator Stephen Mallory proposed an understanding. So long as Buchanan did not strengthen Slemmer's position, the gathering Florida militia would not attack it. The president agreed.

By the time Major Anderson (too late) informed Buchanan that his relocated garrison now needed no immediate assistance, the president had also ordered the merchant steamer *Star of the West*, carrying troops and supplies and bravely flying the Stars and Stripes, to set sail from Brooklyn for Charleston. Warned (traitorously?) of the ship's mission by Secretary of the Interior Jacob Thompson of Mississippi, Charleston's batteries drove off the unarmed ship on January 9. Had another man occupied the White House, we might date the Civil War from that attack's first shot, fired by Citadel cadet George Haynsworth. Anxious to avoid war, the president made no further attempt to reinforce the forts before handing the problem to Lincoln. Equally reluctant to act, the two Southern governors soon placed the forts' fate in the hands of the government forming in Montgomery.

⁓ The Congress that assembled in Washington on December 3 to consider the presidential message seemed ill suited to its task.[6] Elected two years earlier, many of its members had already been voted out of office. Though secession's momentum called for timely action, Republicans hoped that nothing vital might be surrendered before Lincoln's inauguration. Further complicating matters, Democrats controlled the Senate by a wide margin, and Republicans fell short of the combined strength of the lower body's collection of Democrats, Americans, and Whigs. Because secession had transformed a highly symbolic confrontation over slavery in the territories into a crisis of governance, the weakened Congress also faced an unprecedented challenge. To satisfy secessionists, it somehow had to go beyond traditional legislative compromise to deny an incoming administration the prerogative of implementing its electoral platform.

How could Congress possibly overcome such obstacles in the three months of legislative life remaining to it? Did a compromise satisfying both Republicans and the Deep South even exist? Mississippi's Senator Albert Brown suggested that it did not: "The crisis can only be met in one way effectually . . . and that is, for the northern people to review and reverse their whole policy upon the subject of slavery." Though many Republicans remained open to limited concessions, few would maintain the Union by yielding to the South effective control over the Lincoln administration. Nor would the new president, as he told visitors to Springfield, redefine his or his party's principles sufficiently to suit secessionists. Doing so, he claimed, "would make me appear as if I repented for the crime of having been elected, and was anxious to apologize and beg forgiveness."[7]

Despite such difficulties, Congress moved ahead by fits and starts. Virtually ignoring Buchanan's message, the House promptly created a Committee of Thirty-three (one member from each state) charged with finding ways to preserve the Union. During meetings held between December 12 and January 14, Republicans on the committee defended their party platform while trying to reassure the upper South that slavery was safe where it already existed. Two provisions of the committee's resolution-packed, five-part report revealed Republican efforts to prevent further secession. Bending his party's platform a bit, Charles Francis Adams of Massachusetts proposed immediate statehood for New Mexico along with its slave code and twenty-four slaves. With the upper South in mind, committee chairman Thomas Corwin of Ohio offered a constitutional amendment protecting slavery against congressional interference within a state.

After a two-week Senate debate over creation of a similarly charged Committee of Thirteen, Kentucky senator John Crittenden broke the deadlock on December 18 when he introduced a package of seven amendments and four resolutions. Finally established, the committee, with only five Republicans, met from December 22 to 31 before acknowledging a stalemate. Even so, the Crittenden Compromise became the basis of later deliberations in both the House and Senate and the Peace Conference that met in Washington during February. Who was this senator who so shaped the debate over compromise? And what had he proposed?

〜〇 Like Jefferson Davis and Abraham Lincoln, about to become the era's principal antagonists, John Crittenden, its major conciliator, was born to an ambulant father whose family occupied a Kentucky log cabin.[8] Grandson of a midseventeenth-century English immigrant to Virginia, Crittenden's father grew to maturity in North Carolina. He left there at age twenty-one to survey trans-Appalachian land claims and, later, serve in Revolutionary War units commanded by Daniel Morgan and George Rogers Clark. After the war he returned to Virginia long enough to marry before settling near Lexington, Kentucky, where the couple raised nine children and acquired several thousand acres and seventeen slaves.

For young John Crittenden, his parents provided a first-rate education: boarding school, legal training, and graduation from the prestigious College of William and Mary. From his studies, Crittenden emerged with a fine mind, oratorical skills, and influential friends: two cousins of Chief Justice John Marshall, future Jackson adviser Francis Blair, future president John Tyler, and the father of 1860 presidential candidate John Breckinridge. Soon thereafter, Crittenden also acquired a well-connected wife, a relative of the Lees of Virginia and of General and future president Zachary Taylor. Crittenden's principles, moderation, and congenial manner also won for him the admiration of Congressman Lincoln and the friendship of Mary Todd Lincoln's father. Needing only military service to round out the résumé of a successful frontier politician, Crittenden served with distinction in the War of 1812. Thus grounded, he moved quickly to the political forefront, at one time or another serving as state legislator, speaker of the state house, U.S. district attorney, U.S. senator, attorney general to Presidents William Henry Harrison and Millard Fillmore, governor of Kentucky, and member of the U.S. House of Representatives.

Though a Southerner owning nine household slaves, Crittenden held to the Jeffersonian view that slavery constituted "a great evil."[9] Giving substance to his principles, he had voted in 1833 to bar the importation of slaves into Kentucky and, while in Congress, joined fifty other members in an address praising the American Colonization Society and soliciting funds for its work. Even so, Crittenden opposed immediate and forcible emancipation as likely to do great harm. Confident that Nature had imposed limits on the spread of slavery, Crittenden regarded the debate over its territorial status as insubstantial and pernicious, an issue that should not endanger the Union. He had a point. In 1860 the territories of New Mexico and Utah, which had enacted slave codes nearly a decade earlier, possessed fewer than thirty slaves each. As Crittenden told voters, there was no "one single spot of any considerable extent in any Territory . . . where any man would desire to carry his slaves." Americans had no good reason, then, to put the Union at risk by fighting over "what is to be done when the people carry their slaves where they don't want to carry them."[10] Why, he implied, should the North insult the South by doing through legislation what Nature already forbade? And why should the South provoke the North by demanding slavery's protection where it did not, could not, exist?

Inheriting fellow Kentuckian Henry Clay's mantle as the Great Pacificator, Crittenden denounced sectional provocation in all its forms. He condemned the constitutionally doubtful method by which President Tyler annexed Texas and the way President James Polk had provoked an unrighteous war with Mexico. Attempting to prevent a divisive debate over slavery, Crittenden opposed ending that war with a territorial indemnity. Unsuccessful in that, he favored the immediate admission to the Union of New Mexico and California so that the South might be "beaten" not by imposition of free-soil principles but "in the least offensive & injurious" manner possible. Defeated again, he helped Stephen Douglas push through Congress the Compromise of 1850. Out of office in 1854, Crittenden spoke out against the Kansas-Nebraska Act, and back in Congress he helped Douglas defeat imposition of the proslavery Lecompton constitution. In 1860, when Jefferson Davis presented inflammatory resolutions calling for federal protection of slavery in the territories, Crittenden criticized him for creating "a present evil out of an apprehension of a future one . . . never likely to occur."[11]

Troubled by growing sectional animosity, Crittenden tried to save the Union by drawing conservative nationalists from both sections into the Constitutional Union Party and then by working diligently to put Tennessee's John Bell in the White House. With Bell defeated, Lincoln elected, and secession impending, Crittenden devised the compromise for which he is now best known.

≈ Crittenden's plan for saving the Union had many parts. Its principal constitutional amendment would extend the Missouri Compromise line to California, recognizing slavery in territories to its south and prohibiting it to the north. Only when seeking statehood might residents opt for slavery or freedom. With slavery already established (weakly) in the New Mexico Territory, that proposal seemingly offered little of substance to Southerners—or slavery, which would have been driven from the Utah Territory, which lay north of the line.

One phrase in the amendment, however, held out great promise for the South; it applied the division to all territory "now held, or hereafter acquired." With the possibility of a tropical slave empire in mind, a Texas editor observed that the South would gain not only "new fields of enterprise" but also "the means of carrying into execution some plan by which [it] can restore the lost balance of power [in the federal government]." Because the "Southern States cannot afford to be shut off from all possibility of expansion toward the tropics," Breckinridge considered the "hereafter" clause vital.[12]

According to historian Robert May, Southern interest in a tropical slave empire had recently become a divisive sectional issue. The clause consequently put Crittenden's entire package in a bad light and provided an additional reason for its rejection by angry Republicans. Even a later modification requiring that both Southern and Northern majorities approve annexation of new territory failed to reassure them. Surely, Lincoln predicted, "A year will not pass, till we shall have to take Cuba as a condition upon which they will stay in the Union. . . . There is, in my judgment, but one compromise which would really settle the slavery question, and that would be a prohibition against acquiring any more territory."[13]

Other features of the compromise produced fewer Northern objections. Four of its remaining six amendments would prohibit abolition of slavery on federal property within a slave state and in the District of Columbia as well as interference with either the interstate slave trade or slavery within a state. The fifth promised compensation to owners of fugitive slaves rescued by Northern mobs, while the final amendment would bar modification of either the proposed amendments or the existing three-fifths and fugitive-slave clauses of the Constitution. Four congressional resolutions rounded out the package. They would strengthen the ban on the foreign slave trade, confirm the constitutionality of the Fugitive Slave Act, declare null and void conflicting provisions of state personal liberty laws, and, in the principal concession to Northern opinion, call for removal of certain of the act's obnoxious clauses.

Could any grievance assuaged by the Crittenden Compromise have peacefully reconstructed the Union? Surely something bigger, something not remedied by tinkering, had driven secession forward. With Republicans determined to prevent the spread of slavery as a means to achieve its ultimate extinction and the Deep South intending to preserve and extend it by means of independence, neither antagonist had much interest in Crittenden's flurry of amendments and resolutions. Perhaps both saw circumstances as Lincoln did: "The tug has to come and better now than later."[14] With South Carolina's secession convention preparing to vote the state out of the Union on December 20, the national crisis had probably moved beyond compromise. Crittenden's backward-looking package only remotely addressed issues now faced by the Union: the legality of secession and the right of a fairly elected president to govern. Both lay beyond the reach of hurried compromise.

～ The search for reconciliation nevertheless continued—in the Senate's Committee of Thirteen, the national Peace Conference, and, in the last week of its life, both houses of the 36th Congress. In addition to Crittenden's amendments and resolutions, the Senate committee considered a proposal by William Seward, presumably presenting Lincoln's views, calling for a constitutional amendment guaranteeing slavery in the states, modifying the Fugitive Slave Act, and repealing Northern personal liberty laws. That proposal could not satisfy the Deep South, and, before the committee acknowledged failure on December 31, both Jefferson Davis and Robert Toombs joined committee Republicans to reject the heart of Crittenden's plan: extension of the Missouri Compromise line.

Unwilling to give up, Crittenden reintroduced his plan in the Senate on January 3 accompanied by an unusual call to submit it to voters in a plebiscite. The Senate could have sent the modified proposal to the House on January 16, despite Republican opposition, had any three of fourteen abstaining Deep and Upper South senators been willing to vote in its support. The extremes had again joined hands, as Douglas believed, because radicals thought that defeat of the compromise would strengthen the hands of secession's advocates in Georgia, Louisiana, and Texas. On January 21 the House began debate on its committee's resolutions. Rejecting both the Crittenden Compromise and immediate admission of New Mexico as a slave state, it approved and sent to the Senate only Corwin's amendment prohibiting congressional interference with slavery within a state.

While Congress struggled, attention focused on the Washington Peace Conference convening in the nation's capital on February 4 in response to a call from Governor John Letcher and the Virginia legislature.[15] Though transportation difficulties accounted for the absence of representatives from the Pacific Coast states, the presence of only twenty-one other delegations did not bode well for sectional compromise. Rather than look to Washington for compromise, the seven Deep South states had sent their delegates to Montgomery to write a new constitution, and three hard-line Republican states—Minnesota, Wisconsin, and Michigan—refused to go anywhere. Other Northern states also considered staying away, but conservative Republicans favored compromise and moderates wished to appear flexible. From within the conference, moreover, they could block unacceptable agreements.

Despite an impressive collection of delegates headed by former president John Tyler, the advanced age of most participants caused it to become known as the Old Gentlemen's Convention. Following opening ceremonies and the selection of a Committee of Twenty-one (one member of each delegation), the conference did little while the committee labored. On February 15, that body submitted two minority reports and a majority recommendation, which called for a single constitutional amendment combining Crittenden's proposals.

After a week of sharp debate, the conference began voting. It made short work of minority reports calling for a national convention in Kentucky and restructuring the federal government to give the South a veto on both legislation and appointments. The conference then took up the many parts of the majority report's single amendment. Addressing first its most controversial section, the conference reversed an early defeat to approve by 9 to 8 the extension of the Missouri Compromise line across the remaining territories. The section requiring concurrent slave and free state majorities for acquisition of new territories then passed by 11 to 8. The remaining sections of the amendment, the rest of the Crittenden Compromise, won by wider margins, and the Peace Conference rushed its recommendations to Congress.

Receiving the report on February 27, a week before the end of the session, the House and Senate once again considered reconciliation. In the House, however, the conference report remained on the Speaker's desk until March 1, when a motion to suspend the rules and debate it narrowly failed to win the required two-thirds majority. The extremes—radical Republicans and secessionist Democrats—both voted against receiving the report.

In contrast, the Senate promptly sent the conference report to a select committee chaired by Crittenden, who returned it favorably the next day. To bring it to an immediate vote, he substituted the Peace Conference's proposed amendment for his earlier bill, which had been before the Senate since January. On the session's last day, a coalition of the extremes, like that in the House, defeated it 28 to 7. After rejecting the original Crittenden proposal as well, about dawn on March 4 the senators gave two-thirds' approval to the Republican-backed House amendment prohibiting congressional interference with slavery within a state.

That could hardly reconstruct the Union, though it might influence the controversy over secession in the upper South.

～ The nation—for the moment—remained at peace, but neither the administration nor Congress had much to show for its labors. In response to the secession of seven states and their formation of a new government, Congress had only sent to the states for ratification an amendment prohibiting congressional interference with slavery within a state, which even Republicans had long acknowledged lay beyond the reach of Congress.

Who was to blame for such insubstantial results? To ask that question presupposes that a real possibility of compromise had existed and that some group failed to find it or another to accept it. To be sure, both parties to the dispute had gravely misjudged the other's intentions. Many Republicans had regarded disunion as a bluff, an attempt to play on Northern fears in order to gain what the South had lost at the ballot box. For their part, Southern radicals believed that faint-hearted and avaricious Yankees would yield rather than risk a war for the Union.

Did such misjudgments really matter? During the fateful winter of 1860–61 the Deep South, refusing to be governed by a party committed to slavery's ultimate extinction, chose independence. In addition to protecting slavery, that step satisfied the region's aggrieved sense of honor—subjected, according to a New Orleans editor, to "*a deliberate, cold-blooded insult and outrage*" by the election of Lincoln. As suggested in a letter signed by thirty Southern members of Congress on December 13, before the search for compromise had really begun, many Southern leaders felt that reconciliation asked more of them than they were willing to risk. "The argument is exhausted," the signers advised constituents. "All hope of relief in the Union, through the agency of committees, Congressional legislation, or constitutional amendments, is extinguished. . . . We are satisfied that the honor, safety, and independence of the Southern people are to be found only in a Southern Confederacy."[16] They soon set about ensuring that would be so.

Having fairly won the election, Republicans refused to abandon their party's platform and yield effective control of the government to those who had lost it and now engaged in a law-less disruption of the Union. That asked too much. As Massachu-setts congressman Adams explained, having "once and for all thrown off the domination of the Slaveholders," Republicans might compromise on many things, but not on the further exten-sion of slavery. We will not, warned Iowa congressman James Grimes, "surrender all our cherished ideas on the subject of sla-very, and agree . . . [to] change the Constitution into a genuine pro-slavery document, and to convert the Government into a great slave-breeding, slavery-extending empire." For the present terri-tories, the issue may have become symbolic by 1861, but Repub-licans remained determined to bring slavery to an end—some day. That principle accepted, much might be accomplished; with-out it, little. It was a question of power, explained Adams. The seceded states would accept "nothing short of [the] surrender of everything gained by the election. . . . They want to continue to rule."[17] Republicans in Congress and Confederates in Montgom-ery had drawn the line. With power, principle, and honor at stake, neither would submit. Could peace somehow be kept while cool heads found a way to recast the issues? That largely depended upon two new presidents.

NOTES

1. Cobb to Augustus Wright, February 18, 1861, quoted in Robert E. May, *The Southern Dream of a Caribbean Empire, 1854–1861* (Baton Rouge: Louisiana State University Press, 1973), 224–25.

2. For more information on the Buchanan administration's efforts to keep the peace and preserve the Union through compromise, as de-scribed in this section of the chapter, see David M. Potter, *The Impending Crisis, 1848–1861* (New York: Harper & Row, 1976), 514–21 and 535–45; Roy F. Nichols, *The Disruption of American Democracy* (New York: Macmillan, 1948), 374–87, 416–29, 439–44, and 470–73; and James M. McPherson, *Battle Cry of Freedom: The Civil War Era* (New York: Oxford University Press, 1988), 246–51.

3. The quotations from Buchanan's message found in this and the following paragraphs are from James D. Richardson, ed., *A Compilation of the Messages and Papers of the Presidents, 1789–1897*, 10 vols. (Washing-ton, DC: By Authority of Congress, 1899), 5:626–28, 630–31, 635, and 638.

4. Buell's instructions to Anderson quoted in W. A. Swanberg, *First Blood: The Story of Fort Sumter* (New York: Charles Scribner's Sons, 1957), 50–51. On the forts see also Richard N. Current, *Lincoln and the First*

Shot (Philadelphia: J. B. Lippincott, 1963), and Kenneth M. Stampp, *And the War Came: The North and the Secession Crisis, 1860–1861* (Baton Rouge: Louisiana State University Press, 1950).

5. Floyd's instructions quoted in Swanberg, *First Blood*, 93. See also Maury Klein, *Days of Defiance: Sumter, Secession, and the Coming of the Civil War* (New York: Alfred A. Knopf, 1997), 149.

6. For more detail on the efforts of Congress to develop a compromise as described in this section see Potter, *Impending Crisis*, 522–35; McPherson, *Battle Cry*, 251–56; and Nichols, *Disruption*, 388–483.

7. Brown and Lincoln quoted in Potter, *Impending Crisis*, 522–23.

8. This sketch of Crittenden's life rests upon the biography by Albert D. Kirwan, *John J. Crittenden: The Struggle for the Union* (Lexington: University of Kentucky Press, 1962).

9. Crittenden quoted in ibid., 344.

10. Crittenden quoted in ibid., 361.

11. Crittenden quoted in ibid., 259 and 345.

12. Jesse L. Keene, *The Peace Convention of 1861* (Tuscaloosa, AL: Confederate Publishing Co., 1961), 119–28, reprints the compromise as proposed by Crittenden in the U.S. Senate on December 18, 1860. On Southern imperialism and its relation to secession see May, *Southern Dream*, 206–44. The editor and Breckinridge quoted on pages 11 and 228. On Southern imperial expansion as a factor in secession and the acceptability of compromise see pages 206–44.

13. Lincoln quoted in May, *Southern Dream*, 219–20.

14. Lincoln quoted in Stampp, *And the War Came*, 186. Pages 1–262 of Stampp's study provide a useful description of the handling of the secession crisis between Lincoln's election and his inauguration.

15. On the peace conference as described herein see Robert G. Gunderson, *Old Gentlemen's Convention: The Washington Peace Conference of 1861* (Madison: University of Wisconsin Press, 1961). For a briefer account of the compromise see Potter, *Impending Crisis*, 530–32.

16. Quoted in McPherson, *Battle Cry*, 231 and 254.

17. Adams and Grimes quoted in Eric Foner, *Free Soil, Free Labor, Free Men: The Ideology of the Republican Party before the Civil War* (London: Oxford University Press, 1970), 223, 222, and 219.

CHAPTER NINE

ABRAHAM LINCOLN, FORT SUMTER, AND THE UNION

In *your* hands, my dissatisfied fellow-countrymen,
and not in *mine*, is the momentous issue of
civil war. The Government will not assail *you*.
You can have no conflict without being
yourselves the aggressors. *You* have no oath
registered in heaven to destroy the Government,
while *I* shall have the most solemn one to
"preserve, protect, and defend it."
—Abraham Lincoln[1]

Firing upon that fort will inaugurate a civil war
greater than any the world has yet seen. . . .
At this time it is suicide, murder, and will lose
us every friend at the North. . . . You will wan-
tonly strike a hornet's nest. . . . It is unnecessary;
it puts us in the wrong; it is fatal.
—Robert Toombs[2]

DESPITE OCCASIONAL (INTENTIONAL?) ambiguity, Abraham Lincoln's March 4 inaugural address revealed his determination to reconstruct the tottering Union while also suggesting his strategy for doing so. To encourage Southern unionists, he referred to "the most ample evidence" of his many speeches denying any intention, "directly or indirectly, to interfere with . . . slavery in the States where it exists."[3] To make that guarantee "express and irrevocable," Lincoln announced his support for the recently proposed constitutional amendment. So long as enforcement of the Fugitive Slave Act protected free blacks from enslavement, Lincoln also promised to continue returning escaped slaves, observing that recapture would not occur "at all" should disunion succeed. While those words might not win over any seceded state, they might undercut further disunion in the upper South.

The president had to do more; he must both reassure the North and remind secessionists that their actions had consequences. To those ends, he stated his conviction that history and logic revealed that "the Union of these States is perpetual." Even if regarded as simply "an association of States" bound by "contract," a view he rejected, "no State upon its mere motion" and without the agreement of "all the parties who made it" could lawfully leave the Union. From "a moral point of view," a state might act without such consent only if "by the mere force of numbers a [national] majority should deprive a [regional] minority of any clearly written constitutional right." That had not occurred, and confident that the seceded states had been granted every right "plainly written in the Constitution," Lincoln challenged them to demonstrate otherwise. Failing that, their ordinances of secession were "legally void," the equivalent of insurrection or revolution, and "acts of violence . . . against the authority of the United States."

Even the *Dred Scott* decision, which he did not name, had established no unmet federal obligation to write a territorial slave code. Though the government must show "very high respect and consideration" for the Supreme Court's decision, it need do so only in regard to "parallel cases." Because parts of the decision touched on territorial slavery issues—"vital questions affecting the whole people"—the government must resist the "political purposes" of those seeking to convert a narrow decision affecting only "the parties to the suit" into the "policy of the government." Court decisions, Lincoln observed, sometimes proved "erroneous" and were "overruled," never becoming a "precedent for other cases." No single, controversial, and limited decision by the Supreme Court should "irrevocably" fix the policy of the government, set aside the popular will, and undemocratically put "Government into the hands of that eminent tribunal."

With such arguments, Lincoln warned the seceded states that they had attempted disunion without justification and in defiance of the majority, "the only true sovereign of a free people," whose rule all men had an obligation to accept. If majorities could not rule, they submitted to the "despotism" of a minority. If they tolerated secession, they opened the way to the "anarchy" of "renewed secession" as new minorities fractured the government rather than bend to the popular will. Rejecting the rule of a constitutional majority consequently represented both an illegal act and bad policy.

Carefully proclaiming his determination to preserve the Union, Lincoln pledged to "hold, occupy, and possess the property and places belonging to the Government, and . . . collect the duties and imposts." Beyond "what may be necessary for these objects," he would not invade or otherwise use "force against or among the people anywhere." Rather than impose "obnoxious strangers" on the South, he would even "forego for the time" filling certain federal offices and, if "repelled," attempting to deliver the mail "in all parts of the Union."

Lest even those limited actions alarm Southerners, Lincoln closed on a moderate note. "We are not enemies, but friends," he reminded them, and "must not break . . . bonds of affection" forged during decades of common sacrifice. Though he would soon swear "to preserve, protect, and defend" the Constitution, the leaders of secession had "no oath registered in heaven to destroy the Government." The "momentous issue of civil war" consequently lay with them. "Nothing valuable can be lost by taking time" looking for "the best way" out of the nation's "present difficulty." To keep the peace while making that search, Lincoln would not "assail" the seceded states; only aggression on their part would lead to war.

Hidden in that moderation—and Jefferson Davis could hardly have missed it—lay Lincoln's determination, peacefully if possible, to maintain the Union. Playing for time, the new president would avoid precipitate action while filling federal offices, establishing his administration, and implementing his party's platform. That done, the Deep South might abandon secession. If not, the Union could better accept the blow if an unwanted clash occurred. For the moment, the president would do no more than deliver the mails, collect duties on goods entering Southern ports, and hold onto forts still in the government's possession.

Lincoln surely anticipated that those policies would put his Confederate counterpart in a bind.[4] Denying the Montgomery government certain symbols of its independence (the forts) and limiting the exercise of its sovereignty (collecting tariffs) would reveal its impotence. Some supporters already grumbled: What sort of government cannot control its territory, regulate its foreign trade, or even deliver its mails? If Montgomery tolerated such limitations, it would encourage Southerners to abandon the Confederacy, and the demonstration of its impotence might destroy its slim chances of European recognition. The Confederate alternative—a violent assertion of its sovereignty—also served the Union's interests. If Davis attacked the forts, the Confederacy would bear the onus of aggression even as its assault united the Union and yielded to it the moral high ground that Davis had sought to occupy by disingenuously asserting a federal denial of state's rights—not preservation of slavery—as justification for secession.

〜 Many things about Lincoln's background shaped his inaugural, and a sketch of his life will reveal the origins of his thinking and his policies. Born in 1809 in slaveholding Kentucky to parents whose families had migrated from Virginia, Lincoln spent his youth in that part of Indiana settled by Southern migrants.[5] As an adult in central Illinois, he, like Stephen Douglas, maintained Southern ties while living where migration from the slaveholding South met the stream of new arrivals with roots in antislavery New England. The future president strengthened his links to the South in 1842 when he wed Mary Todd, the daughter of a wealthy Kentucky banker, merchant, and slaveowner.

Those associations probably account for Lincoln's moderation and his refusal to condemn slaveholders as evil people. As he told Southerners in an 1859 Cincinnati audience, "I think Slavery is wrong, morally, and politically. . . . I desire that it should gradually terminate in the whole Union. . . . I understand you differ radically with me upon this proposition." That difference voters should resolve in a fair election. In the meantime, "We mean to remember that you are as good as we are; that there is no difference between us other than the difference of circumstances. We mean to recognize and bear in mind always that you have as good hearts in your bosoms as other people, or as we claim to have, and treat you accordingly."[6] Next year, when Lincoln became his party's presidential nominee, few Southern leaders acknowledged such sentiments or refrained from vilifying him.

Though sympathetic to the South, Lincoln claimed that he had opposed slavery for as long as he could recall, an assertion supported by parental influence and youthful experience. Thomas, his father, shared the poor white farmer's resentment of planters who bought up the best land and forced men of his class to compete with bound labor. From both his parents (and his stepmother), who attended a Separate Baptist church, Lincoln would have heard slavery condemned as un-Christian. His relations with his father soon gave substance to what young Lincoln had heard about slavery's evils. An impoverished farmer, in bad health and having eight mouths to feed, Thomas Lincoln allowed his son only a year's schooling before putting him to hard labor in the fields. Always needing cash, Thomas regularly hired out his son to neighbors and kept the lad's wages. From that experience, and the way his father punished his inattention to work and ridiculed his fascination with books, Lincoln acquired great empathy for the plight of slaves.[7] He knew how it felt to be degraded, denied an education, put to work at hard labor, robbed of his wages, and subjected to frequent beatings.

To escape such treatment, Lincoln left home promptly at twenty-one and for the next seven years earned his living in and around New Salem, Illinois, as riverboat man, carpenter, store clerk, merchant, postmaster, blacksmith, surveyor—and state legislator. After months of self-study, he was admitted to the bar in 1837 and moved to Springfield. Riding from town to town to try cases throughout the Eighth Judicial Circuit and handling appeals before the state supreme court, Lincoln quickly became known as a lawyer's lawyer, eventually earning the then-sizeable income of $5,000 per year, investing in real estate, and marrying into a prominent family.

Lincoln's rise from poverty and ignorance to the ranks of the comfortably self-employed and socially respected epitomizes the Republican Party's free-labor ideology and accounts for the enthusiasm with which he defended it against slavery's challenge. As he frequently reminded audiences, "at an early age, I was myself a hired laborer, at twelve dollars per month." So long as opportunity remained open, Lincoln maintained, no man with "two strong hands" and "a heart willing to labor" need spend his life working for others. After a few years in another person's employ, that man might buy land, start a family, hire others, and raise his standing. For Lincoln, the best of the United States was its society of prosperous farms and villages, of economically independent, socially respected, self-made men who set an example for poor men to follow. To keep open opportunities for the lowly, both native born and recent immigrant, free-labor society must expand. Should slavery reach into the territories, however, it would establish aristocratic government, close off the working man's hopes of advancement, and deliver a killing blow to "the liberal party throughout the world." Slavery constituted more than "injustice" to the slave; it was "bad policy" for the nation.[8]

∽ Lincoln's views on free-labor society, like those of most Northerners, merged easily with his commitment to maintain the Union. As he told the young men of an Ohio regiment passing through Washington during the Civil War, "I happen temporarily to occupy this big White House. . . . I am a living witness that one of your children may look to come here as my father's child has. It is in order that each of you may have through this free government . . . an open field and a fair chance for your industry, enterprise and intelligence[,] that you may all have equal privileges in the race of life . . . , [that] this struggle should be maintained, that we may not lose our birthright."[9] Upon the Union's survival, then, depended the future of free-labor society and man's opportunity for advancement.

Despite the many material reasons to oppose secession, Lincoln regarded his ideals as the Union's most compelling argument.[10] So had many others, for the president's views keenly reflected long-standing tradition linking the Union's preservation not only to prosperity and individual progress but also to America's global role as liberty's champion. Almost three decades earlier, in another inaugural delivered near the end of another crisis, Andrew Jackson had predicted that "loss of liberty, of all good government, of peace, plenty, and happiness, must inevitably follow a dissolution of the Union." Moving beyond politics, influential Unitarian minister and pamphleteer William Ellery

Channing called attention to a divine preference for Union when he described the nation as "called by Providence to a twofold work—to spread civilization over a new continent, and to give a new impulse to the cause of human rights and freedom." In the mid-1850s even Jefferson Davis had extolled the Union as a "brotherhood . . . binding and perpetual." Its "light illumines . . . [the] path" of all who seek liberty.[11]

If Americans had a duty to preserve an unbreakable Union, to whom was it owed? Themselves surely, but also to the nation's Founders, posterity, the world, and, as Channing implied, to God. In "The Building of the Ship," Henry Wadsworth Longfellow gave poetic voice to those obligations:

> Sail on, O Union, strong and great! . . .
> Humanity with all its fears,
> With all the hopes of future years,
> Is hanging breathless on thy fate!
> We know what Master laid thy keel
> What Workmen wrought thy ribs of steel.

Nor did only ministers and poets praise the Union. In the judgment of historian Paul Nagel, a quarter century's advocacy of an unbreakable Union had by 1860 made New York senator William Seward its leading defender. Speaking of the American global mission, Seward had declared the Union "the ark of safety in which are deposited the hopes of the world." The Union also ensured "blessings upon us and our posterity" and meant "glory more imperishable than Grecian or Roman fame." Without the Union "the desolation of tyranny will cover these plains; the curses of posterity will fall upon us, and the last experiment [in self-government] thus ended: for men there will be no more political redemption till the last trumpet shall sound, to call the nations to their last account."[12]

In 1861, then, many Americans anticipated economic ruin, social collapse, despotism, and global disgrace should they sacrifice their destiny by breaking the Union. With so much at stake, Lincoln and Northerners believed that secession could not possibly represent the will of the South. Surely those who promoted disunion were a minority—insincere, possibly traitorous, maneuvering for political advantage. Surely Southerners would soon come to their senses. If not, how could Lincoln fail to oppose them?

∼ As Lincoln took the oath of office, secessionists did not hate him for loving the Union—at least not yet. Rather, they had demonized Lincoln the candidate and now feared Lincoln the president because of his position on slavery. They did so despite his Southern roots and his sympathy for Southerners ensnared by an immoral relationship with their bondmen but fearful of the economic and social consequences of setting them free. During four terms in the Illinois legislature and one term in the U.S. Congress, moreover, Lincoln rarely expressed open opposition to slavery. With the Missouri Compromise limiting slavery's extension, as he thought intended by the Founders, Lincoln said little and confidently anticipated its eventual extinction. In light of widespread negrophobia, that was a safe course. Any criticism of slavery that had branded him an abolitionist would likely have ended his political career.

Events soon blasted Lincoln out of his lethargy and back into the maelstrom of politics, from which he had virtually retired at the end of his congressional term in 1849. The 1854 Kansas-Nebraska Act's repeal of the Missouri Compromise caught him "by surprise" and left him "astounded . . . thunderstruck and stunned." He abandoned hopes that the Compromise of 1850 had "settled forever" the status of slavery in the territories, ensuring its ultimate, if gradual, extinction. After a few months of reflection, he took to the stump, speaking out against "the great wrong and injustice of . . . the extension of slavery into free territory." Then came the 1857 *Dred Scott* decision, convincing Lincoln that a Slave Power dominated the federal government, including the Supreme Court. "We shall *lie down* pleasantly dreaming that the people of *Missouri* are on the verge of making their State *free*," Lincoln warned the 1858 Illinois Republican convention, "and we shall *awake* to the *reality*, instead, that the *Supreme* Court has made *Illinois a slave* State." The nation, he predicted, could not forever endure "half *slave* and half *free*. . . . It will become *all* one thing, or *all* the other."[13]

Thereafter speaking boldly, Lincoln depicted slavery as "a vast moral evil," a violation of the nation's "*central idea*"—equality and the opportunity to rise. Every man, black and white, he said, had the right to eat "the bread that his own hands have earned." Chief Justice Roger Taney might challenge the clear meaning of the Declaration of Independence, secessionists might call its proclamation of equality a "lie," and proslavery advocates might extol the superiority of Southern civilization and advocate bondage for all who labored, but Lincoln would defend liberty to the fullest. He acknowledged that blacks had not been equal to whites in 1776, or, for that matter, all whites to one another. He nevertheless maintained that the Declaration had established the "standard maxim for free society." That standard was one "familiar to all, and revered by all; constantly looked to, constantly labored for, and even though never perfectly attained, constantly approximated, and thereby constantly spreading and deepening its influence, and augmenting the happiness and value of life to all people of all colors everywhere."[14]

⁓ The morning following Lincoln's inauguration, a symbol of the Union—Fort Sumter's garrison—and not the future of slavery became the new president's paramount concern. To his considerable dismay, Major Robert Anderson had just advised an amazed secretary of war that he must surrender his command if not provisioned within six weeks. In a flash, the major had ruined Lincoln's plan to play for time and peacefully overcome the Confederacy by undermining its claims of sovereign independence. In addition to blighting Lincoln's strategy, Anderson's unexpected announcement put at risk the president's inaugural pledge to hold the forts. It now seemed likely that the Confederacy would take Sumter, the pre-eminent symbol of federal authority, without firing a shot.

Dismayed and at times uncertain, Lincoln still held to his promise not to abandon the forts. He faced down General Winfield Scott, his military secretaries, and five cabinet members when they recommended withdrawing the Sumter garrison. To do so, Lincoln later explained, would "discourage the friends of the Union, embolden its adversaries, and go far to insure to the latter, a recognition abroad." That "could not be allowed"; it "would be our national destruction consummated."[15] Unwilling to accept Scott's estimate that Sumter's relief required a fleet of warships and twenty-five thousand nonexistent troops, Lincoln again ordered him to hold the forts, a task now accompanied by instructions to land the soldiers whom President Buchanan had held aboard the *Brooklyn*, waiting offshore at Pickens. Able to land them without resistance, Lincoln would not stand idly by as Confederates prepared to overwhelm the Florida fort at their convenience.

William Seward, the new secretary of state, caused bigger problems even than Scott had. Insensitive to Northern opinion, Seward pressed Lincoln to withdraw from the forts in order to preserve the loyalty of the upper South and allow time for unionists elsewhere to turn back secession. To the same ends, Seward urged other, even fantastic, schemes on the president: initiating a foreign war might bring the seceded states back into the Union; appointing a Virginian to the Supreme Court might reassure doubtful Southerners; abandoning Fort Sumter might enable Virginia unionists to guarantee their state's loyalty. Lincoln several times offered to make that swap—a fort for a state—but the Virginians always misunderstood his proposition, turned it aside, or demanded further concessions.

That much Seward did openly. In his indirect dealings with the three commissioners sent by Montgomery to negotiate Confederate recognition and surrender of federal property, the secretary ignored his president's policy. Hoping to prevent precipitate action, Seward repeatedly held out to the commissioners the prediction that Lincoln would soon evacuate Sumter. Aware that he might be deceiving them, they appeared to accept his assurances because President Davis wished to check Union reinforcement while his government completed the ring of artillery batteries under construction around Sumter. Even within the administration, Seward was less than straightforward. He urged Scott to make the excessive military estimates that for a time convinced some cabinet members to favor withdrawal, and his secretive meddling in naval affairs took from the Sumter expedition a warship essential to its success.

While Seward schemed, Lincoln struggled to honor his inaugural pledge. How was he to relieve Sumter before Anderson's mid-April deadline? To answer that question, Postmaster General Montgomery Blair—son of Jackson adviser Francis Blair, West Point graduate, and Maryland politician, the only cabinet member with military experience—brought to the White House his brother-in-law, Gustavus Fox, an Annapolis graduate, former naval officer, and author of a plan that Buchanan had rejected. Made of sterner stuff than his predecessor, Lincoln refined Fox's proposal to carry supplies to the fort using unarmed sailors manning small boats towed to the fort, at night, by tugs. To demonstrate that he intended no more than providing "food for hungry men," Lincoln decided to forego secrecy, warn South Carolina's authorities of the attempt, and pledge not to land troops so long as the state's forces did not resist the delivery of provisions.[16] Only if the Confederates resisted would warships accompanying the expedition shoot their way into the harbor and land both troops and supplies.

Presented with a plan that did not initiate hostilities or require months of preparation, in mid-March, the cabinet wavered in its support for withdrawing the garrison. To push things along, Lincoln tested his advisers' assumptions about the strength of Southern unionism and the state of Northern public opinion. From Fox and two others sent to Charleston, he received confirmation of the relief plan's feasibility and evidence that Seward's reliance on Southern unionism had no foundation. South Carolina, Lincoln learned, had no interest in reconstruction, and it would as readily fire on a supply vessel as on a ship of war. The surrender of Sumter would, moreover, immediately prompt the Confederacy to demand Pickens and two forts in the Florida Keys. Having measured Northern opinion, Wisconsin Republican Carl Schurz advised: "Reinforce Fort Sumter at all hazards and at any cost!" If you yield Sumter, he warned, "you are as dead politically as John Brown is physically. You have got to fight."[17] Withdrawing the garrison, Lincoln concluded, would gain him little but a share of Buchanan's disgrace.

On March 29 most of the cabinet came over to the Lincoln-Fox plan. If South Carolina allowed supply ships to pass, the Sumter garrison might indefinitely hold its position, thus weakening Confederate claims to sovereign independence and allowing Lincoln to resume playing for time. If the Confederates fired on the provisioning, then they became aggressors in any subsequent war, uniting the North, possibly holding the upper South in the Union, and surely undermining their attempt to pose as innocent victims of federal assaults on state's rights. With Seward still opposed and two cabinet members waffling, the rest now stood with the president. As Secretary of the Treasury Salmon Chase concluded, "If war is to be the result I perceive no reason why it may not be best begun in consequence of military resistance to the efforts of the administration to sustain troops of the Union stationed, under authority of the Government, in a Fort of the Union, in the ordinary course of service."[18]

His plans finalized, on April 4 Lincoln ordered Fox to sail as early as the 6th. On that day the president sent messengers to Anderson, urging him to hold on until the 12th, and to South Carolina governor Francis Pickens, advising him of the intent to provision Sumter. After passing through a gale, Fox, aboard the steam transport *Baltic*, arrived off the entrance to Charleston Harbor at 3 A.M. on April 12. To his dismay, only the lightly armed revenue cutter *Harriet Lane* awaited him. Unknown to Fox, one of the three steam tugs needed to tow the boats carrying supplies had never sailed, and the storm had blown the others to seek safety in Wilmington and Savannah. Nor did he know that Seward's meddling had sent to Fort Pickens his most powerful ship, the *Powhatan*, which had on board the sailors and small boats needed to move the *Baltic*'s supplies.

If the Lincoln administration had acted uncertainly and in haste in preparing its expedition, Confederate planning had been long and deliberate. In one of its first acts, the Confederacy's Provisional Congress had resolved on February 15 to obtain Forts Sumter and Pickens, by negotiation if possible but by force if necessary. Though the Davis government thereafter appeared inactive, to its supporters' frustration, it only played for time while building the artillery batteries essential to Sumter's speedy reduction. If Lincoln shot first, that would be fine, but the Confederates intended to attack as soon as their commander in Charleston, Brigadier General Pierre G. T. Beauregard, announced his readiness. On April 8, when President Davis learned of Lincoln's intention to deliver provisions, he called up more troops and ordered Beauregard to prevent Sumter's resupply. Two days later, he told his general to reduce the fort unless Anderson agreed to immediate surrender. Alone in the cabinet, Robert Toombs, Confederate secretary of state, regarded that move as a fatal blunder; Davis and the others saw only advantages. Striking Sumter would reinvigorate citizens beginning to condemn his inactivity and, they believed, incite secession in the upper South.

When Anderson refused to surrender, Beauregard ordered the batteries ringing Sumter to commence firing at 4:30 A.M. on April 12, with Virginia fire-eater Edmund Ruffin igniting one of the assault's first shots. Hearing the exchange of cannon fire, the highly agitated and very frustrated Fox awaited the arrival of two warships: the *Pawnee*, which appeared about 6 A.M., and the *Pocahontas*, which showed up early the next day. Believing that the ships in view just offshore formed part of a larger force, Anderson and his men stood to their guns. They did so for thirty-four hours—until Confederate fire had set their "fire-proof" barracks aflame, destroyed Sumter's main gates, damaged the weakest section of its walls, blocked access to the powder magazine, but amazingly caused not a single casualty. When Louis Wigfall, Texas fire-eater turned colonel, acting under a flag of truce but on his own authority, rowed out to the fort at midday on April 13, he persuaded Anderson to surrender. Unknown to the major, Fox intended to make a do-or-die attempt to run in supplies that night. To him, completely dispirited by the surrender, fell the duty of transporting Anderson's garrison out of Charleston Harbor.

As Toombs had predicted, the Confederate attack united the North. "The whole population, men, women, and children," observed a Harvard professor, "seem to be in the streets with Union favors and flags." In previously pro-Southern New York City, a quarter of a million people rallied, and a merchant reported that the "change in public sentiment here is wonderful—almost miraculous." A woman wrote that it "seems as if we never were alive till now; never had a country till now." Nor were all those supporting Lincoln Republicans. Democratic standard-bearer Stephen Douglas assured his erstwhile opponent: "Our Union must be preserved. . . . Partisan feeling must yield to patriotism. I am with you, Mr. President, and God bless you." When Lincoln consoled Gustavus Fox, he reminded the dejected former naval officer that they had "both anticipated that the cause of the country would be advanced by making the attempt to provision Fort Sumpter [sic], even if it should fail." Though it had, Lincoln found

it "no small consolation now to feel that our anticipation is justified by the result." He might more accurately have described it
as a very great consolation. The North had taken ranks solidly
behind its president, and the Confederacy stood unmasked "before the civilized world," Fox proclaimed, "as having fired upon
bread."[19]

Just as Davis had attacked in the belief that his assault would
draw the states of the upper South into the Confederacy, Lincoln
had anticipated that violent Southern resistance to supplying
Sumter would unite the North. By reducing the fort even before
that attempt could be made, Davis made his government doubly
the aggressor—at least in the minds of Northerners already
outraged by secession, the seizure of so much federal property,
and months of inaction in Washington. Even so, historian Kenneth Stampp rightly concluded that Lincoln had not set out
to provoke war but rather to enforce the law and secure federal
property.[20]

Subsequent events offer evidence of Lincoln's limited aims.
Responding on April 15 to the attack on Sumter, he called for
only seventy-five thousand ninety-day militiamen, perhaps
enough to defend Washington for a time but hardly a sufficient
force to invade the Confederacy, which already had more men
under arms. On April 24 the president acknowledged his peaceful intent to Rudolph Schleiden, minister from Bremen and dean
of Washington's diplomatic corps, who received Lincoln's permission to attempt peace negotiations. Commenting on the
Confederacy's April 17 declaration of war, even Davis implicitly
acknowledged Lincoln's moderation when describing the Union's
aim as "capturing its fortresses."[21] On that same day, however,
Davis escalated the conflict when he offered letters of marque,
making privateers of ship captains, whatever their nationality,
willing to raid the Union high-seas commerce. Two days later,
Lincoln announced a naval blockade of Confederate ports. Not
until the end of April, however, did he begin insisting that Northern governors enlist only three-year volunteers, evidence that the
president had at last abandoned hope that blockade and a few
limited sea-borne operations might cause the Confederacy to
yield. By then, Lincoln recognized that he could have peace only
by accepting Confederate independence. Beginning to prepare

for what became an unexpectedly long and bloody conflict, Lincoln told Minister Schleiden to abandon his efforts.

How long and how bloody depended on the number of upper South states joining the Confederacy. As calculated by historian James McPherson, those eight slave states grew three-fifths of the entire South's food crops and possessed two-thirds of its white population, three-fourths of its industry, one-half of its horses, and three-fifths of its livestock.[22] How many of those states would now secede, thus weakening the Union and strengthening its adversary? Would secessionists again capture the moment and hurry more Southerners out of the Union as they had done in the Deep South following Lincoln's election?

NOTES

1. From Lincoln's first inaugural address, with his emphasis, reprinted in James D. Richardson, ed., *A Compilation of the Messages and Papers of the Presidents, 1789–1897*, 10 vols. (Washington, DC: By Authority of Congress, 1899), 6:11.

2. Confederate Secretary of State Toombs quoted in William C. Davis, *"A Government of Our Own": The Making of the Confederacy* (New York: Free Press, 1994), 310.

3. The quotations from Lincoln's inaugural in this and the following paragraphs are found in Richardson, *Messages and Papers*, 6:5–12. For other useful interpretations of Lincoln's address and his policy as described in this chapter see Richard N. Current, *Lincoln and the First Shot* (Philadelphia: J. B. Lippincott, 1963); James M. McPherson, *Battle Cry of Freedom: The Civil War Era* (New York: Oxford University Press, 1988); and Kenneth M. Stampp, *And the War Came: The North and the Secession Crisis, 1860–1861* (Baton Rouge: Louisiana State University Press, 1950).

4. On this point see also Stampp, *War Came*, 276.

5. On Lincoln's life, career, and politics as described in this chapter see David H. Donald, *Lincoln* (London: Jonathan Cape, 1995), and Stephen B. Oates, *Abraham Lincoln: The Man Behind the Myths* (New York: Harper & Row, 1984).

6. Lincoln quoted in Oates, *Lincoln*, 76–77.

7. Michael Burlingame, *The Inner World of Abraham Lincoln* (Urbana: University of Illinois Press, 1994), 36–42.

8. Lincoln quoted in Donald, *Lincoln*, 234, 177, and 134.

9. Lincoln quoted in Oates, *Lincoln*, 91. On the evolution of American feelings about the Union as described in this section of the chapter see Paul C. Nagel, *One Nation Indivisible: The Union in American Thought, 1776–1861* (New York: Oxford University Press, 1964), and Mark W. Summers, " 'Freedom and Law Must Die Ere They Sever': The North and

the Coming of the Civil War," in Gabor S. Boritt, ed., *Why the Civil War Came* (New York: Oxford University Press, 1996), 177–200.

10. For the North's material arguments on behalf of the Union see Stampp, *War Came*, 204–38.

11. Jackson, Channing, and Davis quoted in Nagel, *One Nation*, 169, 148–49, and 154. See also ibid., 112–13.

12. Longfellow and Seward quoted in ibid., 216–17 and 106.

13. Lincoln, with his emphasis, quoted in Donald, *Lincoln*, 167–68, 170, 208, and 206.

14. Lincoln, with his emphasis, quoted in Oates, *Lincoln*, 71 and 74. See also ibid., 68–70.

15. Lincoln quoted in Donald, *Lincoln*, 287.

16. Lincoln quoted in McPherson, *Battle Cry*, 271.

17. Schurz quoted in Current, *First Shot*, 118–19.

18. Chase quoted in ibid., 80–81.

19. Citizens quoted in McPherson, *Battle Cry*, 274; Douglas in Donald, *Lincoln*, 280; Lincoln in Current, *First Shot*, 175; and Fox in Stampp, *War Came*, 285.

20. Stampp, *War Came*, 284–86.

21. Davis quoted in Current, *First Shot*, 162.

22. McPherson, *Battle Cry*, 276.

CHAPTER TEN

ANDREW JOHNSON,
JOHN LETCHER, AND
SECESSION IN THE UPPER SOUTH

Our people [in Louisiana] are calmly and
fully determined never to submit to Lincoln's
administration, or to any Compromise with
the Northern States. . . . Can you explain to me
why there should be such a different state of
feeling in [North Carolina]? Is it not strange,
when the border states suffer so much more
from Northern fanaticism, from actual loss in
their property, and these same states equally
interested in slavery, that a feeling of antagonism
to the North, should be so much stronger [in
the Gulf States]? I cannot understand it.
—William Clark[1]

WILLIAM CLARK CONFESSED his lack of understanding in a January 1861 letter to his nephew Lewis Thompson, scion of a family of wealthy North Carolina planters and owner of the Louisiana plantation on which his less successful uncle lived. In asking for an explanation of the Upper South's behavior, Clark revealed just how poorly citizens of the Deep South understood attitudes within the eight slave states to their north. By looking no further than a presumably equal interest in slavery, Clark joined even better placed men in demonstrating how little he knew about the circumstances and feelings shaping behavior outside his region. William Seward, for example, long held an unfounded faith in the strength of Southern unionism, and Jefferson Davis mistakenly expected the Southern sympathies of Northern Democrats to survive his attack on Fort Sumter. Though Clark could not account for it, and it soon frustrated his new nation's leaders, a "different state of feeling" did indeed exist in the eight states of the Upper and Border South, all of which refused to rush pell-mell out of the Union in the wake of Abraham Lincoln's victory.

Lincoln's election to the presidency had roused secessionists everywhere. But by January 1861 unionists had gained tenuous control of the four states of the Upper South as well as the four others along slavery's northern border.[2] They had slowed secession there because of several factors that set their states apart from the Deep South. The most obvious of the differences, Clark's assumption notwithstanding, was the upper South's proportionately smaller stake in slavery. (See Table 2, p. 85.) In the seven states of the Confederacy, blacks made up nearly one-half of the total population, and two-fifths of their white residents lived in slaveowning families. In the states of the Upper and Border South, however, the percentages of blacks fell to 32 percent and 17 percent, respectively, and the proportion of whites with a direct stake in slavery varied from a high of 29 percent in North Carolina to a low of 3 percent in Delaware. Reflecting that difference, in Virginia and the Border South antislavery movements had long challenged if not yet overcome slaveowning interests.

The two hundred thousand free blacks living in the upper South—six times the number in South Carolina and the Gulf States —represented another significant difference. Over 90 percent of Delaware's blacks, constituting 18 percent of the state's total population, were free, while in Maryland the comparable figures were 49 percent and 12 percent.[3] White residents of those states would not easily fall prey to secessionist hysteria about emancipation leading to race war and racial amalgamation.

Geographically defined economic and cultural differences within the states of the upper South also muted the fire-eaters' emotionalism. Whether running along east-west or north-south lines, tension between low-country planters and up-country yeomen troubled most upper South states, provoking hostility toward planter leadership and opposition to secession—if pursued on behalf of slavery. Reinforcing the yeomen were businessmen with Northern economic ties and residents of Northern or foreign extraction living in the states' commercial centers.

Moving beyond tangible differences that set the upper South apart, its vigorous two-party system also helps account for its deliberative approach to disunion.[4] When the national Whig Party collapsed, its Deep South leaders often moved into their state's typically radical Democratic Party. In the upper South, Whig leaders maintained their political base and, running under various labels—American, Opposition, or Constitutional Union Party—contested Democratic domination of their states. When the Deep South made secession an issue, competitive upper South political parties ensured that no claim for disunion's benefits would go unchallenged. Aided by party organization, party newspapers, and voters' traditional loyalties, secession's opponents put their message before the public to an extent unknown in the Deep South. With the Union at stake, moreover, the upper South's Democratic parties began to fracture as antiplanter yeomen abandoned their traditional partisan loyalties to support coalitions formed to defeat secession and drive radical Democrats out of state government.

Because of vigorous party competition, the upper South's voters knew that Republicans had guaranteed slavery in the states where it existed, and they heard men whom they respected challenge radical descriptions of an abolitionist North preparing to flood the South with more John Browns. Realizing that an election lost this year might be won the next, upper South leaders and voters intended to give Lincoln a fair trial even as they explored political combinations that might unseat him. Voters also heard their leaders describe secession as a Democratic conspiracy against the welfare and rights of slaveless yeomen, an argument that fed resentment of planter radicals who were trying to drag their states into a cotton kingdom.

Energetic leadership, too, helps explain the upper South's cautious approach to secession. Its unionists took the offensive and, aided by party organizations and papers, used very Republican arguments to remind voters of the Union's benefits. They pointed out the need to develop their state's economies along Northern lines—a mix of agriculture, industry, and trade—and warned that membership in a free-trading, cotton-dominated Confederacy would preclude diversification. Denying that the federal government had in any way dishonored the South, union-ists challenged opponents to fight for their rights within the Union. Believing above all that disunion meant war with their states as its battlegrounds, upper South unionists struggled to derail secession and achieve a Union-restoring, peacekeeping sectional compromise. To that end, they pressed Lincoln to sur-render the forts and forego provocative efforts to collect tariffs outside Southern ports.

〜 Though unionists slowed the South's postelection stam-pede to the Confederacy, we should not, with Seward, fail to rec-ognize their often-feeble commitment to the Union. That is not to say that the upper South had no unconditional unionists. We now know Tennessee's Andrew Johnson for his 1868 impeach-ment and trial; we might better remember him for the resolve with which he defended the Union and remained loyal while oth-ers fell away. Born in 1808 to a family of poor but respected manual laborers, Johnson was only three years old when his fa-ther died.[5] His mother remarried, but his parents left him un-schooled and later apprenticed both Andrew and his older brother to a tailor. After training for five years—and teaching himself to read—Johnson ran off. Having worked various tailoring jobs in the Carolinas and Tennessee by age fifteen, he reappeared in Ra-leigh in 1826 to help his family move to Tennessee.

After trying several villages in the vicinity of Greeneville, he returned there to open up shop and wed Eliza McCardle, in a ceremony performed by Mordecai Lincoln, Johnson's future po-litical associate and a cousin of Thomas Lincoln, Abraham's fa-ther. Johnson's skill, hard work, business acumen, and educated wife (who helped him with his writing) soon brought prosperity, middle-class status, respect, and election as alderman, mayor, and state legislator. A strong stump speaker whose humble origins won him the loyalty of artisans, small farmers, and mountain-eers, Johnson used public office to champion public education, free homesteads, and an egalitarian Democratic Party. He also exploited his supporters' hostility to Tennessee's slaveowning aristocracy, even though he purchased a few slaves of his own as domestic help.

Supported by the state's yeomen, Johnson served in the U.S. Congress from 1843 to 1853, when the state Democratic Party, aware of his mass appeal, twice made him governor, and he helped it dominate rival Whigs. With control of the legislature, the Democrats sent him to the Senate, where he served, even after his state's secession, until Lincoln made him military governor of Union-occupied Tennessee and, in 1864, his vice presidential running mate.

During the Tennessee debate over disunion, Johnson lambasted secessionists as "traitors" and "vile miscreants." Falsely claiming to advocate secession in defense of the South's honor and its slave property, they were in fact cowards who refused to defend their rights within the Union. Slavery was only their pretext for forming a new government "as far removed from the people as they can get it." Theirs was a "conspiracy" against "the liberty of the great mass of the people." Slaveowning aristocrats had no sincere interest in Northern "guara[n]tees in reference to slavery"; they only claimed to fear the alleged abolitionism of the "free men of the north." Their real dread, asserted Johnson, was rule by "the free men South," who threatened the planter elite's "absolute Control" of government and its schemes to place "the institution of Slavery beyond the reach or vote of the nonslave holder [sic] at the ballot box."[6] With such appeals, Johnson and other upper South unionists drew yeomen Democrats from their traditional loyalties, joined them to new Union parties, and gave them hope of defeating secessionist Democrats in the 1861 elections.

⁓ To Lincoln's great regret few unionists had Johnson's unyielding love of the Union. Most of those working to stall the upper South's drive toward secession practiced a very qualified unionism, one well exemplified by another Democrat, Virginia governor John Letcher. By the time of Letcher's birth in 1812, his father, a former manual laborer, had established himself as proprietor of a general store in Lexington, an area populated by westward-moving Scots-Irish and Germans sliding southward up the Shenandoah Valley from Pennsylvania.[7] Though provided a field-school education and a year at Washington College, Letcher slighted his studies, and his father apprenticed him to a local carpenter. Manual labor soon put the young man in mind of a career in politics and law.

While making several failed attempts to gain a seat in the House of Delegates and Congress, Letcher achieved financial success as a lawyer and public acclaim as a newspaper editor in defending the interests of Virginians living west of the Blue Ridge. As editor, he used the *Valley Star* to promote Democratic candidates and, in the 1840s, demand a more egalitarian state constitution—one fair to Virginia's northwestern counties, which held 55 percent of its white population but only 17 percent of its slaves. By basing representation on total population, slaveowning Virginians elsewhere in the state had kept control of its legislature, in which they wrote tax codes benefiting planters and defeated transportation improvements that would aid northwestern counties. After serving as a delegate to the 1850–51 constitutional convention, where he threatened the state's dismemberment if the legislature did not justly represent his region, Letcher was rewarded by his constituents with the first of four terms in Congress. In 1859 the lawyer-editor-politician and owner of a few household slaves became Virginia's governor-elect.

Aware of the reaction to John Brown's December execution, the new governor used his January 1860 inaugural address to urge sectional reconciliation through a national convention. A loyal Democrat, he condemned radicals who had fractured his party to promote disunion. "Such Marplots* as [William] Yancey," he stated, cared for nothing but "disunion, and the best means of effecting it." Their "Slave Code proposition" had no purpose but destruction of the country's remaining national party.[8] Though Letcher's unionism did not run so deep, he supported Stephen Douglas even after the Little Giant boldly told an audience in Norfolk that secession was an illegal act that he, if president, would meet with force.

When the legislature in January 1861 accepted Letcher's appeal to call what became the Washington Peace Conference and unionists won an apparently overwhelming victory in the February 4 election of a state convention, the governor seemed likely to hold Virginia in the Union. That prospect and Letcher's union-

*Meddlers who interfere with a plan or undertaking.

ism began to fade, however, when the seven Deep South states refused to attend the Peace Conference, Congress rejected significant compromise, and Lincoln failed to surrender Fort Sumter.

Those developments led Letcher to promote a conference of the upper South states. If it worked out an accommodation with the North—and Lincoln allowed the states of the Confederacy to depart in peace—Letcher believed that the Union might be reconstructed (in a few years) when an economically unsuccessful Confederacy of only seven states collapsed. If the conference failed to win concessions, he intended to resist disunion only long enough to create a border confederation. When its member states seceded jointly and later drew the Confederacy to them, the truncated Union would surely make peace with so powerful a combination.

Before that could occur, the Confederacy fired on Fort Sumter and Lincoln called for troops—putting the loyalty of upper South unionists to a test that Letcher's scheming revealed he had already flunked. Moving just ahead of a Southern Rights group planning a coup, many of the Virginia convention's "unionists" joined with radicals on April 17 to vote their state out of the Union. Not much caring who fired first, or that Lincoln's handful of short-service troops foretold no invasion of the Confederacy, they had long accepted that any clash of arms would, by forcing them to choose sides, send them into the Confederacy's eager arms.

Only in the northwest did unionist delegates stand firm. Those from Letcher's own Valley rejected disunion by a comfortable margin and representatives living northwest of the Shenandoah defeated it by 6 to 1. Even as secession won overwhelming statewide approval in the May 23 referendum, northwestern voters rejected disunion by 3 to 1. With few slaves and linked economically to Ohio and Pennsylvania, the northwest opted to dismember the aristocratic state that had so long ignored its interests. Under the protection of a Union army, it declared its leaders the loyal government of Virginia, sent representatives to Congress, and approved separation of the new state of West Virginia.

Most unionists in the other states of the Upper South soon revealed that they too lacked the commitment of Andrew Johnson or the West Virginians. In the end, they loved the South more than the Union; and, opposing Northern coercion more than Southern secession, they remained loyal only until compromise seemed impossible. If there was to be war and they must choose sides, most would go with kith, kin, and slavery. Border South unionists would pursue a different course, but Tennessee, Arkansas, and North Carolina joined the Confederacy.

Following the Deep South's secession, Tennesseans thinking slavery an economic necessity sympathized with the Confederacy. Others followed the example of their state's greatest hero, President Andrew Jackson, who had fiercely defended the Union in 1832 when South Carolina nullified federal law. Stiffened by east Tennessee's unionism and doubts about the ability of an untested Confederate government to protect both slavery and their liberties, Tennesseans temporized. Their strategically located state and its agricultural and human resources remained within the Union —for the moment.

When Governor Isham Harris, pursuing his own preferences, tried to rush Tennessee out of the Union, his legislature agreed to an election of delegates only if voters could also decide whether the convention might meet. Roused by the speeches of Andrew Johnson and the editorials of Whig editor William Brownlow and hopeful that the Washington Peace Conference would produce a compromise, the voters supported unionist candidates by a 3-to-1 margin on February 9. That same day, opponents of holding a secession convention won by a margin of twelve thousand votes.

Weakened by rumors that Lincoln would evacuate Sumter and that the Confederacy would fail to submit its constitution to a popular referendum, radicals floundered until the attack on the fort and Lincoln's call for troops made secessionists of many conditional unionists. In a special session called for April 25, the Tennessee legislature rejected a convention and executed a coup by declaring their state's independence. Even so, voters later approved secession by a 2-to-1 margin on June 8. Only in Johnson's east Tennessee did the vote favor the Union, and that region might have followed the separatist path of West Virginia had not Governor Harris used arrests, Confederate troops, and executions to intimidate local unionists. His actions nevertheless sparked a re-*

gional civil war that continued until the Union captured Chatta-
nooga at the end of 1863. Earlier, however, in 1862, a federal army
maneuvered Confederate forces out of Nashville, putting the governor and his legislature to flight and allowing Lincoln to make
Andrew Johnson the state's military governor.

Deep South secession also divided Arkansas. In the state's
south and east, low-country planters, typically recent arrivals
from the cotton states, might have achieved immediate secession
but for the resistance of the mountainous north and west, settled
by yeomen out of the upper South. Though negrophobic, the yeomen stood by the Union because they hated planters, regarded
secession as a slaveowners' plot, blamed them for breaking up
the Democratic Party, and worried lest secession remove troops
on the state's often lawless border with the Indian Country. Beyond the Ozarks, however, Arkansas unionists wanted slavery
protected and opposed secession only in anticipation of an eventual compromise. If conflict forced them to choose, they would
become Confederates.

Though Arkansas had given its electoral votes to John Breckinridge in November, its people took Lincoln's election calmly
and hoped for reconciliation. To that end, its new Democratic governor, Henry Rector, briefly favored a national convention but
soon came out for immediate secession, and his legislature set
February 18 as the date for an election modeled on the Tennessee
plan—selection of delegates accompanied by a referendum on
holding a convention. When secessionists threatened to seize the
Little Rock arsenal unless the governor demanded its surrender,
such lawlessness discredited their cause on the eve of the election. Nonetheless, Arkansas voters allowed the convention to
meet, and vigorous party competition helped unionist candidates
win the delegate vote count by a 4-to-3 margin. When the convention assembled on March 4, unionists used their five-vote
majority to defeat both a secession ordinance and recognition of
the Confederacy before accepting a resolution calling for an August 5 referendum on secession. Following the attack on Sumter
and Virginia's secession, the convention hastily reassembled. On
May 6, by 55 to 15, it rejected a motion to put secession to the
voters and by 65 to 5 took Arkansas out of the Union.

As elsewhere in the upper South, Lincoln's election produced no immediate secessionist majority in North Carolina, where geographic and class divisions checked the influence of slaveholders whose raw numbers exceeded those of every Deep South state save Georgia. With a few exceptions, secession's strength lay in the slaveowning counties of the coastal plain, though not along the coast itself, and in the area around Charlotte. In the piedmont and the mountains, a population of slaveless artisans, yeomen farmers, and antislavery religious sects fueled hostility to "Southern Rights" when that meant "the rights of the slaveholder."[9]

Party competition also checked disunion. Doubting that Lincoln would or could do much harm, North Carolinians opposed being dragged into a confederacy dominated by arrogant, Deep South extremists or into a war bringing higher taxes and military despotism. Even though six states had left the Union by January 29, when the North Carolina legislature approved a convention, secessionists had to compromise to get the needed two-thirds vote. The election might take place no sooner than February 28, and its referendum must authorize the convention to meet, in any case no sooner than March 11. If it met and favored secession, that recommendation would require voter approval. As scheduled, North Carolina went to the polls but to the radicals' dismay narrowly rejected a convention and elected a unionist majority of delegates.

That outcome represented no lasting triumph; Old North State unionism had its limits. One North Carolinian correctly assessed attitudes in his state and elsewhere in the Upper South: "You cannot unite the *masses* of any Southern State much less those of N[orth] C[arolina] against the Union & in favor [of] slavery *alone*." If secessionists changed the issue to the "doctrine of *force*," they could make unionists choose between "*toryism*" and "a Southern Confederacy."[10] When Lincoln called for troops following the attack on Fort Sumter, he helped secessionists change the issue, and North Carolina's support for the Union evaporated. Governor John Ellis called his legislature into special session on May 1, and it directed the previously elected delegates to assemble on May 20, at which time they voted their state out of the Union.

The Confederacy that would contest with the Union for its independence had now reached its fullest extent. It would have to make its fight without the four slave states of the Border South.

∼∽   Those states are another study in complexity. Their first settlers had given them a Southern culture and a Southern economy. Plantation slavery, though a dying institution in each one, persisted in portions of all of them, along with antislavery movements. Also challenging planter influence were the states' large Northern- and foreign-born populations and commercial activities linking their cities to the North by proximity, river, and rail. Nor would the divided states make an entirely free choice; their great strategic importance drew both the Union and the Confederacy into their affairs. Hating secession, emancipation, and coercion, the four states wanted most of all to avoid becoming battlegrounds fought over and ravaged by contending armies. Policies likely to produce that outcome seemed far from obvious.

In Delaware, Governor William Burton and residents of his state's southernmost counties, which contained 90 percent of its tiny slave population, favored the Confederacy. They could not, however, overcome the influence of the du Pont family, the state's vulnerability to federal attack, and New Castle County's large antislavery population of foreign immigrants, Northerners, and free blacks. With the products of its flour, cotton, and gunpowder mills traded through Philadelphia and Baltimore, Delaware awaited Maryland's decision on secession.

That state too had strong material and emotional links to the Confederacy in its southern counties and on its Eastern Shore, where slaves made up 40 and 20 percent, respectively, of the population. Though Maryland's Democratic legislature also favored the Confederacy, slaveowning governor Thomas Hicks refused to call it into session because he preferred to leave the Union only for a middle confederacy of border states. Nor could Maryland prudently secede until Virginia had first done so.

Opposed to disunion in any form were the state's yeomen and antislavery German immigrants of the northern and western counties. Eventually backing them up were Baltimore merchants who doubted that they could survive Confederate free trade or hostile Union control of their rail and sea links to Northern markets. In Washington sat Lincoln, who must hold Maryland lest secession isolate his capital.

Unable to do more, Maryland secessionists formed military companies and awaited an opportunity to act. That time seemingly came when the Sixth Massachusetts Regiment, responding to Lincoln's call for troops, marched through Baltimore on April 19. As the regiment headed for Washington, a mob attacked it with bricks, paving stones, and pistols, and an exchange of shots left dead and wounded on both sides. Within days, locals dropped key bridges and cut the city's rail and telegraph lines, threatening to leave Washington undefended against the army of recently seceded Virginia. Ben Butler, commander of the Massachusetts brigade, was not so easily thwarted. Deftly sending his remaining regiments to Annapolis by steamship, he quickly reopened that city's rail line to Washington. By April 25 federal troops again flowed into the capital; others took up artillery positions overlooking Baltimore, where the government declared martial law.

Hicks finally called his legislature into session, but in unionist Frederick rather than in occupied Annapolis. Its members condemned Lincoln's policies and flirted with a declaration of neutrality and recognition of the Confederacy but made no attempt to secede. The president in turn kept the peace by avoiding confrontation in Baltimore and allowing Confederate recruiters to operate freely. More provocatively, he also suspended the writ of habeas corpus, and Union officers quietly rounded up suspected secessionists. That brought on a clash with Chief Justice Roger Taney, who ordered their release from prison. Such was Taney's reputation in the North that Lincoln's refusal did the president little harm. With calm restored and secessionists silenced, Maryland's June elections gave victories—and three-quarters of the votes—to the six unionist candidates for Congress.

Kentucky, the birthplace of Lincoln and Davis, possessed a five-hundred-mile Ohio River border with the North, and its Cumberland and Tennessee rivers provided logistical systems for offensive operations into Tennessee and Alabama. In pursuit of another state he must have, Lincoln proved the better suitor. Several factors helped his courtship. Though only Virginia and Georgia had more slaveowners, Kentucky had few plantations and relatively few slaves (20 percent of the population). A strong antislavery movement, the regular departure of slaveowners for new lands, and the annual sale of bondmen south had put the institution into decline, and rising commercial interests opposed disruption of their links to the Union. Even many of the state's largest planters accepted the Union because the Fugitive Slave Act ensured the return of their runaways, and its majority of slaveless farmers and the residents of its eastern highlands remained intensely loyal.

As much as most Kentuckians resisted secession, they also condemned coercion and supported the compromise efforts of John Crittenden. When reconciliation made little progress, Governor Beriah Magoffin called the legislature into special session for January 17. In a three-month political struggle, it refused to call a convention but reconvened on May 6 in response to the firing on Fort Sumter and Lincoln's call for troops. Reassured by Lincoln's promise not to invade Kentucky so long as it upheld federal law, both the legislature and the governor proclaimed neutrality.

Though refusing formal recognition of that stance, Lincoln overlooked the state's trade with the Confederacy and in other ways strengthened its unionism with his tolerance. Kentucky's secessionist governor then inadvertently helped the Union cause with his unsuccessful scheming to seize control of the State Guard and the Frankfort arsenal. In the June congressional elections, unionist candidates consequently won 70 percent of the votes and nine of ten seats, a victory that they repeated in the August legislative elections.

Two Confederate blunders then ended Kentucky's temporary neutrality. On August 30, the Confederate Congress appropriated $20 million for seizing the state, and five days later General Leonidas Polk, on his own clumsy initiative, sent troops to occupy Columbus. By the time that General Ulysses S. Grant countered by taking Paducah, Kentucky rested securely in the Union. Demanding that the Confederacy withdraw its troops, the state's legislature also denied Governor Magoffin control of his administration and declared John Breckinridge an outlaw for abandoning his Senate seat and accepting a Confederate commission.

Similar Union patience might as easily have secured Missouri, which had voted overwhelmingly for Stephen Douglas and John Bell in November 1860. When Governor Claiborne Jackson and his secessionist legislature nevertheless tried to push Missouri out of the Union, voters rejected Jackson's insistence that they "stand by [their] sister slave-holding states" to whom they were bound by "common origin, pursuits, tastes, manners and customs"—a statement that must have amused the large German population of St. Louis. [11]

After a 4-to-1 victory that filled the Missouri convention with unionists, Jackson and his legislative allies pursued secession by other means. While the governor put the state's militia under secessionist command and ordered it to assemble for training just outside St. Louis, the legislature placed that city's police force, local militia, and sheriff in secessionist hands. Continuing preparations for a coup, Jackson's supporters seized the small arsenal at Liberty, and on May 8 he received from the Confederacy a requested shipment of the cannon and ammunition needed to take the St. Louis arsenal.

Jackson had not counted on the equally ruthless opposition of Frank Blair, Jr., brother of Lincoln's postmaster general, and Captain Nathaniel Lyon, whom Blair had schemed to put in command of the federal arsenal in St. Louis. To strengthen their hand and cut possible losses, Lyon mustered several of the city's German American regiments into service and secretly arranged with the Illinois governor to transport a large portion of the arsenal's arms and munitions to safety in his state. Ready now to tackle their foes, Lyon's troops surrounded the governor's militia encampment on May 10 and obtained its surrender. Overreaching, Lyon then caused a riot by provocatively marching his prisoners through St. Louis.

Drawing no useful lesson from behavior that pushed some conditional unionists into the governor's camp, Blair and Lyon plunged ahead. Rejecting a truce, they moved on Jefferson City and put the governor and legislature to flight. Having found temporary sanctuary in the state's southwest corner, the Missouri government approved an ordinance of secession. Its unionist convention meanwhile declared itself the state's legitimate government and elected new executive officers. Though the Union now controlled the state, willful men and violent ways had over-whelmed moderation and prompted a brutal civil war that limited Missouri's support for the Union.

~~~ The fifteen slave states had made their choices. The war for the Union—and Confederate independence—had begun. Four years later, Lincoln used his second inaugural address in a search for its meaning. He speculated that the nation's most bloody war ever represented divine punishment for the slavery that both sections had so long tolerated. If so, it might be God's will that the war continue "until all the wealth piled by the bondsman's two hundred and fifty years of unrequited toil shall be sunk, and until every drop of blood drawn with the lash, shall be paid by another drawn with the sword." From so harsh a retribution, Americans must not flinch; for, "it must be said, 'the judgments of the Lord, are true and righteous altogether.' "[12] For the war, understood as divine punishment for slavery, all Americans bore responsibility; and, in a sense never intended by William Seward, the conflict had indeed been irrepressible.

NOTES

1. Clark to Lewis Thompson, January 10, 1861, quoted in Daniel W. Crofts, *Reluctant Confederates: Upper South Unionists in the Secession Crisis* (Chapel Hill: University of North Carolina Press, 1989), xvi. Crofts mistakenly placed Clark in Alabama.

2. In addition to Crofts's study, cited above, covering North Carolina, Tennessee, and Virginia, this chapter rests on the following: Jonathan M. Atkins, *Parties, Politics, and the Sectional Conflict in Tennessee, 1832–1861* (Knoxville: University of Tennessee Press, 1997); Jean H. Baker, *The Politics of Continuity: Maryland Political Parties from 1858 to 1870* (Baltimore: Johns Hopkins University Press, 1973); Steven A. Channing, *Kentucky: A Bicentennial History* (New York: W. W. Norton, 1997); Marc W. Kruman, *Parties and Politics in North Carolina, 1836–1865* (Baton Rouge: Louisiana State University Press, 1983); Paul C. Nagel, *Missouri: A Bicentennial History* (New York: W. W. Norton, 1977); Allan Nevins, *The War for the Union*, vol. 1, *The Improvised War, 1861–1862* (New York: Charles Scribner's Sons, 1959); Henry T. Shanks, *The Secession Movement in Virginia, 1847–1861* (Richmond, VA: Garrett and Massie, 1934); J. Carlyle Sitterson, *The Secession Movement in North Carolina* (Chapel Hill: University of North Carolina Press, 1939); James M. Woods, *Rebellion and Realignment: Arkansas's Road to Secession* (Fayetteville: University of Arkansas Press, 1987); and William C. Wright, *The Secession*

Movement in the Middle Atlantic States (Rutherford, NJ: Fairleigh Dickinson University Press, 1973).

3. Calculated from data assembled in Table 2 on page 85.

4. On the importance of party competition to a state's reaction to Lincoln's election see Michael F. Holt, *The Political Crisis of the 1850s* (New York: John Wiley & Sons, 1978).

5. On Johnson see Hans L. Trefousse, *Andrew Johnson: A Biography* (New York: W. W. Norton, 1989).

6. Johnson quoted in ibid., 134, and Crofts, *Reluctant Confederates*, 158.

7. On Letcher see F. N. Boney, *John Letcher of Virginia: The Story of Virginia's Civil War Governor* (Tuscaloosa: University of Alabama Press, 1966).

8. Letcher quoted in ibid., 96, and Crofts, *Reluctant Confederates*, 158.

9. Sitterson, *North Carolina*, 22.

10. C. B. Harrison quoted in ibid., 191.

11. Jackson quoted in James M. McPherson, *Battle Cry of Freedom: The Civil War Era* (New York: Oxford University Press, 1988), 290.

12. Lincoln quoted in James D. Richardson, ed., *A Compilation of the Messages and Papers of the Presidents, 1789–1897*, 10 vols. (Washington, DC: By Authority of Congress, 1899), 6:277.

Epilogue
Some Thoughts on
Alternatives and Consequences

I, John Brown, am now quite certain that
the crimes of this guilty land will never be
purged away but with blood.
—John Brown[1]

Because I love the South, I rejoice in the failure of
the Confederacy. Suppose that secession had been
accomplished? Conceive of this Union as divided
into two separate and independent sovereignties!
. . . Slavery was enervating our Southern society
and exhausting . . . Southern energies.
—Woodrow Wilson[2]

HAD THE MEN of secession and civil war known just how much
blood would flow, they might have thought the price too high.
They might have found some way to avert the nation's drift toward destruction, either by abandoning a Southern confederacy
founded on racial slavery or by fracturing a Union built on free
labor. Applying modern standards, and with nothing personally
at risk, we may wonder that they failed to compromise—or to
yield. Judging by antebellum norms, however, we may better
sense what had to be sacrificed and more clearly appreciate the
unthinkable choices that they faced.

When the men of secession, hoping for peaceful separation
but confident of easy victory, pursued independence, they un-
wittingly put at risk what they most wanted to protect. Implicitly, at least, they accepted war as less threatening to slave society
than a Republican administration committed to the gradual elimination of their peculiar institution. The imminent dangers of war
seemed less fearful than those of a distant future, even one that
might be avoided with a victory at the next national election.

Many explanations have been offered for that judgment. Perhaps they risked war over the right to take their slaves into the territories. The *Dred Scott* decision had already granted that, though without producing any westward shift of slavery. As for the protection of state's rights, a common theme in the years since 1861, the only other right in question seemed to be ownership of human beings, which Republicans had repeatedly promised to guarantee, if only where it already existed. There, slavery might have rested secure, free from external assault. In the same way, poor enforcement of the Fugitive Slave Act seems a odd justification for Southern independence. Thoughtful men would hardly risk war over a failure to return the one in five thousand slaves—most of them from the Border South—who annually fled to safety in the North. Independence, moreover, eliminated any possibility of recapturing runaways.

Moving beyond insubstantial issues, the feared loss of the South's equal place within the Union might better explain secession. In a process begun well before Lincoln's nomination, however, Southern radicals themselves had undermined the effective equality that their section had long enjoyed, despite its numerical inferiority. Though long a minority in the House of Representatives and the Electoral College, the South had nevertheless dominated federal politics by means of its skillful use of national political parties. Yet well before Lincoln's close-won victory, radical Southerners had destroyed both parties. By demanding more of Northern politicians than they would give, radicals first shattered the Whig Party and then gave a Southern sectional character to the Democratic Party, the last remaining instrument of Southern control. Compounding that, but in order to justify secession, William Yancey and company then split the Democratic Party and blasted hopes of electing another pro-Southern president. As a means to achieve independence, radicals had already sacrificed the South's influence within the federal government. Only utter Northern submission, if even that, could have stayed their hand.

In searching further for something to explain acceptance of secession's risks, we might settle on disunion as a defense of Southern honor. To ease psychic injury associated with abolitionist attacks on slavery, however, Southerners could turn to men such as George Fitzhugh, who reminded them that their peculiar institution sustained a society far superior to the North's. Feeling little embarrassment over slavery, all Southerners but extremists and the hypersensitive surely found it easy to ignore distant insult, in any case hardly worth a war.

The dream of a tropical slave empire capable of preserving slavery indefinitely provides a more tangible explanation for what drove secession forward. Both fire-eaters and some moderates had hoped for such a future, and perpetual slavery would enable the South to avoid the horrors assigned to emancipation by secessionists. However appealing, pursuit of a slave empire might have entailed even greater risks than civil war. Seizing slavery's expanded domain might lead to endless conflict—in the Caribbean with European powers refusing to yield colonial dominion, in Latin America with nations unwilling to forfeit their independence or see slavery reestablished where it was already banned, and in the American West with a truncated Union defending its possessions. Secessionists may not, of course, have given any more thought to such matters than they did to the possible costs and outcomes of civil war.

In the year before the Confederate attack on Fort Sumter, well-informed men, both North and South, described secession as the work of conspirators who had first sought destruction of the Democratic Party and the election of Lincoln. Old Whigs and new Constitutional Unionists John Crittenden and John Bell had charged conspiracy. So had Stephen Douglas, his Georgia supporters Alexander Stephens and Herschel Johnson, and, not surprisingly Abraham Lincoln himself and Republicans long suspicious of a Slave Power conspiracy.

Perhaps secession was the work of a conspiracy, one whose methods induced a sort of Southern paroxysm. Yancey, with support from men such as Barnwell Rhett, had schemed to destroy the Democratic Party in 1860. Radicals then worked to defeat unionist candidates Stephen Douglas and John Bell even as they demonized Republicans, rehearsed the terrors of emancipation, and spread exaggerated stories of abolitionist plots and slave insurrections. They thereby prepared the ground for a hasty, unthinking response to Lincoln's election—secession's immediate justification. Pushing ahead while the fear raged, radical governors had sent commissioners to hasten enough separate state secessions to create a viable confederacy. To make turning back difficult, radical legislators helped those governors anticipate disunion by purchasing arms, expanding their militias, and, often before disunion occurred, seizing federal properties. Though not a fire-eater creation, formation of the Confederate government abused the democratic process because some Southern leaders feared that voters might reject their efforts.

Though not denying that fire-eater scheming created fear and a popular need to act, belief in conspiracy must confront the fact that the radicals failed to establish a directed multistate organization to promote secession in a coordinated manner and pursue it in furtherance of a common plan. An independent-minded group of men more obsessed than thoughtful, fire-eaters had often proceeded with a variety of ideas about the best route to their destination. When their states approached secession, moreover, less extreme leaders coming late to secession quickly took control and finished the work of disunion. That done, moderates led the establishment of the new government. Nor must we forget that Southern majorities, even if stampeded into secession, signaled their approval in various ways. Fire-eaters had paved the way, but the public generally approved, and moderates had completed the road to independence. As to the charge of conspiracy, much depends upon how we define it.

We are left to conclude that secession is best understood as a radical-inspired emotional reaction, a paroxysm for which one can offer reasons but no truly satisfactory explanation. We can identify who laid the foundation, created the circumstances, and breathed life into the process. Disunion then seemed to acquire a will of its own, drawing less extreme men into its swirl of emotion and moving them forward in hasty, ill-considered actions responding more to their hopes than any assessment of the costs and risks of independence. The closest thing to a reasoned debate of disunion's consequences took place north of the Deep South. Even there, it only partially delayed secession until another crisis—the attack on Fort Sumter and Lincoln's call for troops—so shook residents that many believed that they must choose between the Union and their Southern brothers.

All readers may not happily trace secession to public acceptance of the fire-eaters' exaggerated descriptions of the South's fate within the Union and their encouragement of an overwrought response to circumstances that they had created. Surely, however, few people will deny that disunion ended in an unparalleled disaster for the eleven states of the Confederacy. However achieved, independence proved for them an appallingly bad choice—a decision too quickly made by men giving little thought to consequences and too weakly resisted by others more sensitive to its dangers. Although that calamity argues for compromise as the better option, at least for the South, we must inquire if some sectional understanding existed, one that Republicans could accept and Southerners would not regard as sounding their doom.

～ By the time of Lincoln's inauguration, many Republicans seemed ready to tolerate slave codes in New Mexico and Utah and organization of the remaining territories on the basis of Popular Sovereignty. What more could they do for the South there? Kansas had demonstrated that even a pro-Southern federal government could not force slavery on an unwilling population. Nor did the Republican offer of a constitutional guarantee of slavery where it existed, a substantial commitment, satisfy the South's honor or interests as the radicals defined them. To their mind, slavery had new fields to conquer in Latin America, hence Southern support for the Crittenden Compromise's "hereafter" clause. In rejecting the clause, Republicans saw it as a source of unending threats of disunion should they oppose future imperial expansion on behalf of slavery. Only some limits on slavery's extension would satisfy them, and that the Deep South would not accept. Moreover, had not the sectional confrontation become, by 1861, the right of a fairly elected president to implement his party's platform rather than one concerning the territories? The Deep South could hardly deny that, or the North yield it.

In contemplating the fevered months before the attack on Sumter, we are right to wonder whether compromise ever had much chance. After years of abolitionist criticism and John Brown's attempt to ignite slave insurrection, Southerners accepting Fitzhugh's views on the superiority of slave society seethed with indignation and fear. When Chief Justice Roger Taney abused both history and the Constitution on behalf of slavery and John Breckinridge maneuvered to force slavery into Kansas, both confirmed for many Northerners the existence of an aggressive Slave Power aiming to make slavery a national institution. In an atmosphere of fear and mistrust, Americans forgot what they had in common. They instead felt repelled and threatened by those living on the other side of the line that separated slave states from free.

In such an environment, radicals made enemies of the Union's advocates, men such as John Bell and Andrew Johnson, and all who would save it through compromise, such as Stephen Douglas and John Crittenden. As secession's influence mounted, leaders across the South's political spectrum—Jefferson Davis, Alexander Stephens, and John Letcher—abandoned support for compromise and helped lay the foundations and define the extent of the Southern confederacy. Ignoring the moderation of men such as Salmon Chase and Abraham Lincoln, Southerners preferred to vilify even advocates of order and constitutional process. If acceptable compromise existed, men who hated and feared their fellow citizens on opposite sides of the Mason-Dixon line were not likely to find it.

~~~ With Southerners fearful and compromise unlikely, should Lincoln have avoided dreadful war by letting the Confederacy go in peace, perhaps in hopes of some distant reunion? He had tried to play for time in hopes of peaceful reconstruction. Unlike Jefferson Davis, who risked war in order to preserve slave society, Lincoln did not embrace a war for its destruction. For him, limiting slavery's spread would suffice because that would reserve the new territories for free workingmen and, he believed, eventually prompt the slaveholding states to end a practice that more than any other violated the nation's most fundamental principles. But, in playing for time, Lincoln found his hand trumped by the attack on Sumter.

That assault put to the test his oath to "preserve, protect, and defend" the Constitution as well as his commitment to secure federal property and maintain the Union. For the president and his party, the Union represented liberty and prosperity, a debt to

posterity, and the obligation to prove that men could govern themselves—imprecise commitments, perhaps, but surely matters of
no less consequence than the preservation of slave society.
Lincoln's former Democratic rival certainly thought so. After the
Confederacy fired on the American flag flying over Sumter, Douglas told a cheering Chicago crowd: "There are only two sides to
the question. Every man must be for the United States or against
it. There can be no neutrals in this war, *only patriots—or traitors.*"[3]
Douglas would stand with the patriots.

How do we judge, knowing the Civil War's destructiveness,
whether the Union was worth the price? We might join with
Woodrow Wilson, at the time a University of Virginia graduate
student, in estimating the cost—in lives, treasure, and blighted
hopes—of a broken Union and a North American continent con-
sisting of a half-dozen petty states struggling for dominance. We
must also assess the Republican contention that destruction of
the Union would undermine democratic government, both in the
United States and abroad. We must finally put in the balance the
radicals' hope that Southern independence would preserve slavery indefinitely and young Wilson's belief that the institution
enervated the region that he so dearly loved. Though fully mind-
ful of the war's great cost, we might apply to the Civil War the
Duke of Wellington's observation about Waterloo and conclude
that "such a victory" as the Union gained in 1865 was but the
"next greatest misfortune to losing."[4]

Before judging too harshly those who fought to preserve the
Union, we might also recall British writer C. V. Wedgwood's observation: "History is lived forwards but it is written in retro-
spect. We know the end before we consider the beginning and
we can never wholly recapture what it was to know the beginning only."[5] Had they known war's costs and outcome, the
men of secession and war might well have avoided the drift toward destruction. Our problem is not knowing which of them
would have been the first to turn aside and submit to the demands of the other. What if the men with the better cause had
been the first to surrender their principles? Might slavery have
endured for generations had Lincoln acquiesced in the Union's
destruction or saved it by supporting imperial expansion in Latin
America?

NOTES

1. Brown's last statement quoted in *The Dictionary of Quotations*, 2d ed. (London: Oxford University Press, 1966), 85.

2. Wilson's graduate-student address quoted in Thomas J. Pressly, *Americans Interpret Their Civil War* (New York: Free Press, 1962), 199.

3. The presidential oath quoted from the U.S. Constitution, Article II, Section 1; Douglas, with his emphasis, quoted in James M. McPherson, *Battle Cry of Freedom: The Civil War Era* (New York: Oxford University Press, 1988), 274.

4. Arthur Wellesley, Duke of Wellington, quoted in *Oxford Dictionary of Quotations*, 564.

5. C. V. Wedgwood, *William the Silent* (London: Jonathan Cape, 1967), 35 and 212–14.

BIBLIOGRAPHICAL ESSAY AND RECOMMENDED READINGS

This essay has two goals: to acquaint readers with the principal works used in the preparation of this book; and, for those wishing to know more, to guide them to more comprehensive descriptions of events and the biographies of individuals associated with the secession crisis of 1859–1861. Dedicated students of the Civil War might select from the titles found in Steven E. Woodworth's *The American Civil War: A Handbook of Literature and Research* (1996), but those simply wishing to place the secession crisis in historical context can do no better than obtain James M. McPherson's very readable *Battle Cry of Freedom: The Civil War Era* (1988) or David M. Potter's *The Impending Crisis, 1848–1861* (1976). Two parts of Allan Nevins's older multivolume study of the war and its origins, *The Emergence of Lincoln*, vol. 2, *Prologue to Civil War, 1859–1861* (1950) and *The War for the Union*, vol. 1, *The Improvised War, 1861–1862* (1959), cover in greater detail the period from John Brown's raid at Harpers Ferry to the post-Fort Sumter secession of the Upper South. Each of the studies mentioned here contributed depth to the interpretation of events offered in the preceding pages, as did Roy F. Nichols's examination of antebellum politics and the Democratic Party, *The Disruption of American Democracy* (1948).

Anyone who wants a less detailed account of the events of 1859–1861 might go to *Secession: The Disruption of the American Republic, 1844–1861* (1990), in which James A. Rawley covers the Civil War's origins in fewer than 150 pages before supplementing his analysis with excerpts from key contemporary documents. A reader wanting to know more about less—namely, events between Lincoln's election and the Confederate attack on Fort Sumter—should read Maury Klein's *Days of Defiance: Sumter, Secession, and the Coming of the Civil War* (1997). Another way to narrow one's focus is to seek a sectional perspective on the events leading to secession through Kenneth M. Stampp's *And the War Came: The North and the Secession Crisis, 1860–1861* (1950), or William L. Barney's *The Road to Secession: A New Perspective on the Old South* (1972).

For the lives of the two principals featured in Chapter One, see Stephen B. Oates's *To Purge This Land with Blood: A Biography of John Brown* (1970) and Frederick J. Blue's *Salmon P. Chase: A Life in Politics* (1987). By clarifying Republican views on the future of slavery and American society, Eric Foner's *Free Soil, Free Labor, Free Men: The Ideology of the Republican Party before the Civil War* (1995) suggests the tragic nature of the Southern misinterpretation of John Brown's raid. Several of the essays in the collection edited by Paul Finkelman, *His Soul Goes Marching On: Responses to John Brown and the Harpers Ferry Raid* (1994), not only describe Southern interpretations of Brown, the abolitionists, and the Republican Party but also reveal Northern reactions to Brown and his raid.

The sketch of George Fitzhugh in Chapter Two draws upon C. Vann Woodward's biographical introduction to Fitzhugh's *Cannibals All! or, Slaves without Masters* (reprint; 1960). A collection edited by Drew Gilpin Faust, *The Ideology of Slavery: Proslavery Thought in the Antebellum South, 1830–1860* (1981), contains extensive excerpts from the writings of the proslavery advocates featured in the chapter. Larry E. Tise, *Proslavery: A History of the Defense of Slavery in America, 1701–1840* (1987), offers just what the title indicates. The twelfth volume, *Proslavery Thought, Ideology, and Politics* (1989), in the collection *Articles on American Slavery* (1989), edited by Paul Finkelman, assembles modern commentary on the thinking of slavery's defenders and promoters. On Roger Taney, see H. H. Walker Lewis, *Without Fear or Favor: A Biography of Chief Justice Roger Brooke Taney* (1965). *Slavery, Law, and Politics: The Dred Scott Case in Historical Perspective* (1981), Don E. Fehrenbacher's abridgment of his earlier masterful study of the *Dred Scott* decision, is all that most readers will need for a full understanding of both the case and the Chief Justice.

The best short supplement to the material in Chapter Three is Eric H. Walther, *The Fire-Eaters* (1992). David S. Heidler, in *Pulling the Temple Down: The Fire-Eaters and the Destruction of the Union* (1994), also assesses their thinking, role, and influence—subjects of later chapters as well. Readers wanting to know more about specific figures can turn to the following: Laura A. White, *Robert Barnwell Rhett: Father of Secession* (reprint; 1965); David F. Allmendinger, Jr., *Ruffin: Family and Reform in the Old South* (1990); Betty L. Mitchell, *Edmund Ruffin: A Biography* (1981); Robert J. Brugger, *Beverley Tucker: Heart over Head in the Old South* (1978); Robert E. May, *John A. Quitman: Old South Crusader* (1985); and Clement Eaton, *The Mind of the Old South* (1964). John McCardell, *The Idea of a Southern Nation: Southern Nationalists and Southern Nationalism, 1830–1860* (1979), puts the entire secession movement in its intellectual context.

Chapter Four rests importantly on *Stephen A. Douglas* (1973) by Robert W. Johannsen, the chapters on William Yancey in Walther's study of the fire-eaters, and Eaton's analysis of Southern thought, both mentioned above. Most readers will find the few existing full-length biographies of Yancey too dated. On the 1860 Democratic convention see the studies by Potter and Nichols and the first of the Nevins volumes.

Potter, Nichols, and Nevins also thoroughly cover the 1860 presidential election, the focus of Chapter Five. Material on Stephen Douglas is found in Johannsen's biography, cited above; for Lincoln biographies, see the paragraph on Chapter Nine, below. For the lives of the chapter's other two principals, see William C. Davis, *Breckinridge: Statesman, Soldier, Symbol* (1974), and Joseph H. Parks, *John Bell of Tennessee* (1950). On the functions of political parties and the contribution of the party system's collapse to the early success of secession, see Michael F. Holt, *The Political Crisis of the 1850s* (1978).

Chapter Six depends on three studies of Southern thought and the secession movement in the Deep South states. Dwight L. Dumond, *The Secession Movement, 1860–1861* (1931); Clement Eaton, *The Freedom-of-Thought Struggle in the Old South* (1964); and Ralph A. Wooster, *The Secession Conventions of the South* (1962) give an overall view of the movement, one supplemented by the Heidler study of the fire-eaters, mentioned above. State studies supplement those works: William L. Barney, *The Secessionist Impulse: Alabama and Mississippi in 1860* (1974); Walter L. Buenger, *Secession and the Union in Texas* (1984); Anthony G. Carey, *Parties, Slavery, and the Union in Antebellum Georgia* (1997); Willie M.

Caskey, *Secession and Restoration of Louisiana* (1938); Steven A. Channing, *Crisis of Fear: Secession in South Carolina* (1970); and Michael P. Johnson, *Toward a Patriarchal Republic: The Secession of Georgia* (1977). Roger L. Ransom, *Conflict and Compromise: The Political Economy of Slavery, Emancipation, and the American Civil War* (1989), provides a helpful economic perspective on Southern secession. Except for the last one, all the works in this paragraph also contribute in some way to understanding the conservatives' failure to hold the Deep South states in the Union. Thomas E. Schott, *Alexander H. Stephens of Georgia: A Biography* (1988), describes the life of the key state's pivotal figure and offers a personal perspective on the shortcomings of Deep South unionism.

Two works by William C. Davis will inform readers wishing to know more about Jefferson Davis and the formation of the cotton confederacy, the subjects of Chapter Seven: *"A Government of Our Own": The Making of the Confederacy* (1994) and *Jefferson Davis: The Man and His Hour* (1991). For more about events preceding the peace efforts featured in Chapter Eight, readers should consult the McPherson, Nichols, Nevins, and Stampp books. Foner's study of the Republicans provides insight into their attitudes and role in efforts to achieve a secession-ending compromise. Those curious about Southern imperialism, a factor in the Republican rejection of John Crittenden's proposals, should go to Robert E. May, *The Southern Dream of a Caribbean Empire, 1854–1861* (1973). Two books, however, provide the foundation of this chapter: Robert G. Gunderson, *Old Gentlemen's Convention: The Washington Peace Conference of 1861* (1961), and Albert D. Kirwan, *John J. Crittenden: The Struggle for the Union* (1962).

Though Lincoln biographies and special studies abound, readers wanting to know more about the principal figure of Chapter Nine should first read David H. Donald's *Lincoln* (1995). Stephen B. Oates's *Abraham Lincoln: The Man Behind the Myths* (1984) and Robert W. Johannsen's *Lincoln, the South, and Slavery: The Political Dimension* (1991) offer detailed analyses of specific issues concerning the Civil War president. The previously mentioned Foner book should help readers wanting to know more about the importance of the Union to Lincoln, Republicans, and Northerners generally, and Paul C. Nagel, *One Nation Indivisible: The Union in American Thought, 1776–1861* (1964), traces the evolution of the concept of Union, revealing its powerful emotional significance. Any of four books might suit readers wanting to learn more about the run up to Fort Sumter and the Confederate attack on the fort: Richard N. Current's *Lincoln and the First Shot* (1963); W. A. Swanberg's *First Blood: The Story of Fort Sumter* (1957); Bruce Catton, *The Centennial History of the Civil War*, vol. 1, *The Coming Fury* (1961); or Stampp's study.

Chapter Ten rests on two biographies and several more state studies. For more on the two principal figures, see F. N. Boney, *John Letcher of Virginia: The Story of Virginia's Civil War Governor* (1966), and Hans L. Trefousse, *Andrew Johnson: A Biography* (1989). The second of the Nevins volumes identified in the essay's first paragraph provides context for the more focused studies of the secession debate in the states of the Upper and Border South. For more on the Upper South, readers should see: Daniel W. Crofts, *Reluctant Confederates: Upper South Unionists in the Secession Crisis* (1989); Jonathan M. Atkins, *Parties, Politics, and the Sectional Conflict in Tennessee, 1832–1861* (1997); Marc W. Kruman, *Parties and Politics in North Carolina, 1836–1865* (1983); J. Carlyle Sitterson, *The Secession Movement in North Carolina* (1939); Henry T. Shanks, *The Secession Movement in Virginia, 1847–1861* (1934); and James M. Woods, *Rebellion and Realignment: Arkansas's Road to Secession* (1987). For more on the rejection of secession in the Border South, they should go to: William C. Wright, *The Secession Movement in the Middle Atlantic States* (1973); Jean H. Baker, *The Politics of Continuity: Maryland Political Parties from 1858 to 1870* (1973); Lawrence M. Denton, *A Southern Star for Maryland: Maryland and the Secession Crisis, 1860–1861* (1995); Steven A. Channing, *Kentucky: A Bicentennial History* (1977); and Paul C. Nagel, *Missouri: A Bicentennial History* (1977).

INDEX

ABOUT THE AUTHOR

The author of *America Arms for a New Century: The Making of a Great Military Power* (1981) and *The American Home Front: Revolutionary War, Civil War, World War I, and World War II* (1983), James L. Abrahamson has had careers in both the U.S. Army and academia. A former professor of history at the U.S. Military Academy at West Point, he later held the Eisenhower Chair at the Army War College and the Barden Chair at Campbell University. He has since been a visiting professor at the University of North Carolina at Chapel Hill and, in retirement, teaches distant-learning courses for the American Military University.